The diocese of Lismore, 1801–69

Maynooth Studies in Local History

SERIES EDITOR Raymond Gillespie

This volume is one of six short books published in the Maynooth Studies in Local History series in 2008. Like their predecessors most are drawn from theses presented as part of the MA course in local history at NUI Maynooth. Also like their predecessors they range widely over the local experience in the Irish past from the middle ages into the twentieth century. That local experience is presented in the complex social world of which it is part. These were diverse worlds that need to embrace such differing experiences as the fisheries of Arklow, or the world of books and reading in Loughrea. For yet others their world was constructed through the tensions which resulted in the murder of Major Denis Mahon near Strokestown in 1847. The local experience cannot be a simple chronicling of events relating to an area within administrative or geographically-determined boundaries since understanding the local world presents much more complex challenges for the historian. It is a reconstruction of the socially diverse worlds of poor and rich, from the poor of pre-Famine Tallaght to the more prosperous world of the Church of Ireland in the diocese of Lismore. Reconstructing such diverse local worlds relies on understanding what the people of the different communities that made up the localities of Ireland had in common and what drove them apart. Understanding the assumptions, often unspoken, around which these local societies operated is the key to recreating the world of the Irish past and reconstructing the way in which those who inhabited those worlds lived their daily lives. As such studies like those presented in these short books, together with their predecessors, are at the forefront of Irish historical research and represent some of the most innovative and exciting work being undertaken in Irish history today. They also provide models which others can follow up and adapt in their own studies of the Irish past. In such ways will we understand better the regional diversity of Ireland and the social and cultural basis for that diversity. If they also convey something of the vibrancy and excitement of the world of Irish local history today they will have achieved at least some of their purpose.

Maynooth Studies in Local History: Number 81

The diocese of Lismore, 1801–69

R.B. MacCarthy

FOUR COURTS PRESS

Set in 10pt on 12pt Bembo by
Carrigboy Typesetting Services for
FOUR COURTS PRESS LTD
7 Malpas Street, Dublin 8, Ireland
e-mail: info@fourcourtspress.ie
http://www.fourcourtspress.ie
and in North America for
FOUR COURTS PRESS
c/o ISBS, 920 N.E. 58th Avenue, Suite 300, Portland, OR 97213.

ISBN 978–1–84682–117–2

Printed in England by
Athenaeum Press Ltd, Gateshead, Tyne & Wear.

Contents

Acknowledgments

This short book is an attempt to recreate something of the diocesan life of the Church of Ireland community in the diocese of Lismore before the disestablishment of that church in 1869. I have made no attempt here to deal with the post-disestablishment situation in the diocese because the Disestablishment Act of 1869 represented a rigid and final dividing line seldom paralleled before in history. Such a work is possible because of the rich vein of diocesan and parochial records to say nothing of the parliamentary papers that surveyed the state of the Church of Ireland in the early 19th century. I have drawn heavily on these. Amounts of money given are to the nearest pound.

The research for this book was done in the years 1961–2 when armed with a letter of introduction from Bishop de Pauley I visited all the resident clergy and their churches. Since then some of the source material has been moved to the Representative Church Body Library in Dublin although much remains in local hands, especially the papers of the dean of Lismore. In addition new research has added regional context to this work, most especially Eugene Broderick, 'Waterford's Anglicans: religion and politics, 1819–72', unpublished MA thesis, University College, Cork, 2000.

Since this short book was written there have been striking changes in the ecclesiastical landscape of the diocese. The church of Derrygrath has been demolished. Killaloan, Macollop, Rathronan and Templemichael have been unroofed while Shanrahan (Clogheen) and Ardfinnan are used only for community purposes. Tallow is used for commercial purposes and Clashmore long unroofed has been re-roofed for community purposes. Villierstown chapel still survives and is used for community purposes but its interior has been gutted – some of its furnishings have been moved to Lismore cathedral.

Introduction

The dioceses of Waterford and Lismore include practically the whole county of Waterford with two baronies and portions of two others, in Co. Tipperary and the diocesan area is roughly co-terminous with the territories of the Desii.[1] It is thought that this population group was expelled from Meath in the time of Cormac Mac Airt, that a portion of the group settled in what is now Co. Waterford and from there, shortly before the coming of St Patrick, extended into that part of the diocese now in Co. Tipperary. This came to be called northern Decies as distinct from southern Decies from which it was divided by the Comeragh and Knockmealdown mountains.[2] The honour of introducing Christianity within the tribal area would appear to belong to Declan, the son of a chieftain, and possibly a precursor of Patrick, who established himself on the coast at Ardmore from where he evangelized the surrounding area.[3] The monastery of Lismore, one of the most celebrated centres of learning in Ireland was founded by Carthagh, otherwise McCuda, in 630, but no attempt to define a territorial area under the sole control of one bishop seems to have been made until the synod of Rathbreasail in 1110.[4] Ardmore, alone of the many monastic bishoprics within the area, seems to have had some success in attaining a territorial jurisdiction since the see was not merged into that of Lismore until after the death of Bishop Moelettrim in 1203.[5]

The diocese of Waterford was of comparatively late foundation it was little more than the Danish city and cantred and its bishop was under the jurisdiction of the archbishop of Canterbury. The first bishop of Waterford was consecrated by Archbishop Anselm in 1096. Hitherto the area had been, if not subject to Lismore, then at least under the influence of the coarb of Carthagh at Lismore. Until their union in 1363, the relations between the sees of Waterford and Lismore were marked by constant bickerings and feuds. Although Waterford diocese is of diminutive extent, the possession of the city has always given it an advantage over Lismore whose only large urban centre is Clonmel, the county town of Tipperary but a bad centre for Lismore diocese as a whole. Nevertheless in spite of this 600-year-old union, Lismore diocese has succeeded to a remarkable degree in preserving its separate identity in the organization of the Church of Ireland though not at all in the Roman Catholic arrangements.

Geographically, the diocese has two backbones. Northern Decies is almost identical with the valley of the Suir, with three considerable urban

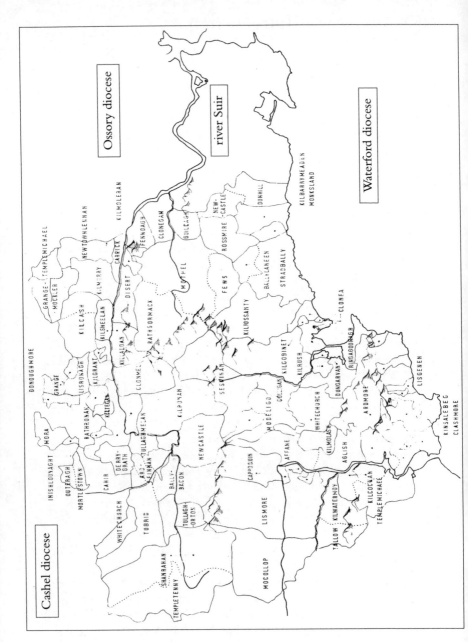

1. Map of Lismore diocese

centres, Cahir, Clonmel and Carrick, placed at intervals of about 13 miles along the north bank of the river. In 1792 Clonmel had flourishing woollen and cotton manufactures and was described as 'large and opulent'.[6] Forty years later the total population was 13,459[7] and the 'church' population was 1,737.[8] As the river was navigable for lighters and barges, a considerable export trade in agricultural products was carried on through the port of Waterford.[9] Cahir with no less than five flour mills in 1837, had a population of 3,408[10] of whom 269 were members of the established church.[11] Carrick, although in a state of decline in 1812[12] had a population of 6,922 in the 1830s[13] but only 235 of these were churchpeople.[14]

The River Blackwater is the main artery of southern Decies. It is tidal as far as the town of Cappoquin. Lismore is only a few miles upstream while the town of Tallow is connected with it by a navigable section of the River Bride. In the 1830s all three had populations between 2,000 and 3,000.[15] Dungarvan, the largest town in the Co. Waterford portion of the diocese, had the advantage of being a natural harbour and a large fishing fleet was based there. In 1831 the total population was 8,386 of whom 335 were members of the Church of Ireland.[16] In the early 19th century Co. Waterford seems to have been in rather a neglected state. Edward Wakefield declared that 'not a gentleman's seat is to be seen between Youghal and the mansion of Lord Waterford at Curraghmore' and that the estates of the duke of Devonshire, the principal proprietor of the county, 'were in a condition disgraceful to a civilized country ... with a few lonely inhabitants who could not speak a single word of English'.[17] Yet in 1792 it was said that the roads were lined with apple-trees and the country covered with orchards.[18]

The 19th century witnessed a unique development in religious affairs in Ireland. For the first and only time the Church of Ireland and the Church of Rome clashed in open opposition. The Irish establishment, 'one of the greatest ecclesiastical anomalies in Christendom',[19] had not hitherto felt any need to assume a missionary character and, in common with Anglicanism elsewhere, had put its trust in the effects of reason and property. The 19th century was marked by the gradual emergence of the Roman Catholic majority as a political force culminating in emancipation in 1829 and thus the established church could no longer trust to the civil power to ensure the quiescence of its rivals while the establishment was itself being transformed and revived by the evangelical movement and fitted for the inevitable conflict. The clash between the two churches for the religious allegiance of the Irish people found issue in two directions: doctrinally in 'the second reformation', a movement for proselytizing the Roman Catholic peasantry especially in the west of Ireland, and organisationally in the seven years tithe war by which the majority protested, on the whole successfully, against having to support the Protestant clergy against its will.

The diocese of Lismore is not usually considered an area in which the second reformation of the early 19th century made much headway but there seems to have been a surprising amount of quiet evangelism carried on all over the diocese. Two families of scripture readers were resident at Tallow and in 1850 a son of Timothy Hourihane of Cappoquin 'Scripture readers' were baptized there. In 1801 a sermon in Irish had been preached in the main street of Carrick by 'a very young saddler' (Methodist) while in 1823 one Ellen Dixon read her recantation in the parish church there before the vicar. In 1824–5 there were classes for adult catechumens (they must have been adults since Ably Knight baptized on 25 November 1827 appears in the classes for 1824). In the latter year there were three classes with a total of 24 pupils. A curious practice was maintained in Clonegam parish. Between 1828 and 1845 there were always one or two entries a year in the marriage register in which both bride and bridegroom were described as 'Roman Catholics'. That they were not converts is demonstrated by a baptismal entry in 1841 in which the parents are designated 'converts'.[20] The established church was charged, probably justly, with using the Famine as an opportunity to further its missionary activity. A clergyman engaged on 'relief' in Co. Tipperary wrote that the Famine 'placed Protestantism before the cottier in a light in which he was never wont to regard it'.[21] He does not record how £700 sent him by readers of *The Gospel Magazine* was disbursed. The town of Carrick was 'adopted' during the Famine by the congregation of the Revd Mr Fenn of Blackheath, and collections of between £30 and £40 weekly was sent to the vicar of Carrick for relief.[22] In 1847 a new curate was appointed for Monksland – a parish in which copper mining was the principal source of employment. There he set up a 'printing school' using child labour and out of the proceeds was able to build a glebe-house.[23] Although the study of the bible was not compulsory yet there was 'a Sunday afternoon bible class and weekday as well as Sunday lectures upon which many of the once unenlightened and prejudiced Romanists voluntarily attend.'[24] Not surprisingly 'the altar rang, the press teemed with anathemas' and many of the enlightened Romanists were turned out of house and home.[25] Still, by 1854 it could be declared that 'a missionary work with all the elements of strength and durability is going forward among the poor Romanists – with the most cheering visible results.'[26] It is difficult to segregate religious and secular education completely even if this is desired and schools at this time depended for their existence on private patronage that in most cases was Protestant and landlord.[27] Thus the introduction of the national system of education in 1835 with 'united secular and separate religious instruction' as its aim[28] was a direct attack on the missionary activity of the Church of Ireland. With the exception of Archbishop Whately, the bishops opposed it and none more strongly than Bishop Daly.

But an enquiry in 1858 into endowed or other independent schools disclosed that the great majority of such schools in the diocese of Lismore were either without pupils or unsatisfactory while those under the national board were uniformly satisfactory.[29] By 1892 most of the Protestant clergy had capitulated to the board.[30]

None of the notorious acts of violence associated with the tithe war appear to have taken place within the diocese of Lismore. In 1832 Dean Dawson of St Patrick's assured Dean Bishopp of Lismore that although 'opposition to tythes and disregard for the laws are the ruling passions just now, yet I understand that in Waterford and in that part of the Co. Tipperary where your property is situated, the People are still paying Tythes'.[31] In 1837 the Roman Catholic parishioners of Ardfinnan sowed six acres of wheat for the curate, Thomas Kettlewell, to mark their gratitude for his humanity in the matter of tithe collection.[32] Nevertheless in this as in other areas of conflict the ultimate victory was with the recently-emancipated majority.

1. The bishops

It is a matter for surprise that Lismore has so successfully maintained its separate identity throughout the 600 years that have elapsed since the union with Waterford. In 1363 the diocese was united with the neighbouring small diocese of Waterford,[1] which itself appears to have been formed out of Lismore diocese in 1096.[2] Probably from the time of this union the bishop's place of residence was usually in the city of Waterford. Later Lismore castle was the residence of the bishops and it was not until the period 1583–9 that Archbishop Miler Magrath, who then held the sees of Waterford and Lismore *in commendamin*, alienated it, together with the manor and see lands, to Sir Walter Raleigh. It was purchased from Raleigh in 1602 by Sir Richard Boyle, later 1st earl of Cork, the restorer of the cathedral church.[3]

The episcopal revenues were large in comparison with those of the parish priests, which is not of course a phenomenon peculiar to the Irish church in the 19th century. In 1810 Waterford and Lismore was returned to the lord lieutenant as being worth £5,000.[4] In 1831 and for three years previously the average net income was £3,934[5] while at the end of the period the income of the four united sees was £4,347.[6] Although it could not compete with the opulence of Derry with £12,159 net a year in 1831, Waterford and Lismore was not the poorest of the Irish sees, and the government preferred to fill it by translation rather than by consecration.[7] The bishops were not, in any sense, salaried. Their income was derived from landed property in the shape of rents and renewal fines, whose collection gave endless vexation and trouble to the bishop and often resulted in diminution from the nominal income.

Bishop Richard Marlay (1795–1802) had been translated from Clonfert. The son of a chief justice of Ireland and uncle of Grattan, he distinguished himself by being one of the only two bishops who voted against the Union.[8] The friend of Burke, Charlemont, Sir Joshua Reynolds and Johnson, he wrote for private theatricals and composed 'some amusing pieces of poetry'.[9] In fact he was 'a person of great talents and universally esteemed as an Excellent Prelate'.[10] There is no evidence, however, that this esteem was gained by any great exertions in his dioceses.[11] Dr Marlay died 'at his seat at Celbridge near Dublin'[12] so it is not surprising that his successor, Trench, found the palace at Waterford in a great state of dilapidation,[13] thus affording him the opportunity of spending £5,000 on it.[14]

Bishop Trench (1802–10) was of a well-connected, landed family in Co. Galway.[15] He had an undistinguished university career[16] and secured the incumbency of his home parish only a few weeks after his ordination to the priesthood in 1792.[17] Although he had no church, he officiated in a room in Ballinasloe, appears to have been active in good works in the parish and kept no curate[18] – an item of self-denial then regarded as a sure sign of zeal on the part of the incumbent. He seems to have been a notable example of the better type 'squarson', and during the rebellion of 1798 he scoured the country night and day hunting the rebels.[19] Even his admiring biographer felt that some apology was necessary for the elevation of this conscientious and charitable magistrate to the episcopal bench at an early age of 32.[20] In fact, the appointment was unashamedly a 'Union engagement.'[21] His brother Richard Trench had voted against the Union in the Irish House of Commons in 1799 but for the measure in 1800. The rewards included a viscountcy and earldom for his father, who as Baron Kilconnell had supported the union in the Lords, and a bishopric for his younger brother.

For the first two years of his episcopate, while the palace was being repaired, he did not reside much in his dioceses.[22] In Dublin, where he now had a house and occasionally lived, he was popular as a preacher.[23] Thereafter he settled down at Waterford where he proved himself an efficient and conscientious administrator.[24] But it was noted that 'he had not that decided religious turn of mind, with which it pleased God to bless him at a future period; but he was a most excellent reader and a most impressive preacher'.[25] He concerned himself with the erection of churches[26] and determined to inspect personally every parish and church previous to his annual visitations. 'He usually travelled on horseback attended by one servant, taking a hired chaise for relief at intermediate stages, and every summer was seen passing through highways and byeways, untrodden before by a Protestant bishop.'[27] The observations which he added to the report which he made in 1807 to the lord lieutenant on the state of his dioceses[28] showed that he possessed an accurate knowledge of the situation and needs of every one of his parishes.[29]

He did not have to wait too long before his family arranged for him to take another step up the ladder of preferment – in this case to the see of Elphin, a move which also had the advantage of taking him back to his own area.[30] A man of strong and masterful character,[31] he was advanced to the archbishopric of Tuam in 1819, where he became one of the foremost figures in the Ireland of his day[32] chiefly because of his connection with the 'second reformation' in western Connacht.[33] His episcopate in Lismore may be counted a success – for his vigorous and practical attitude was needed after the scholarly Newcome and the dilettante Marlay.

It is possible to reach a more definitive estimate of the character of Bishop Joseph Stock (1810–13) than of the other six prelates with whom this chapter is concerned because during his time at Waterford and earlier at Killala he wrote frequently and at length to his son Henry, a proctor in Dublin, and fortunately these letters have survived.[34] A former fellow of

Trinity College and a distinguished scholar,[35] he seems to have owed his elevation to personal merit.[36] His enduring claim to be remembered is that he was at Killala at the time of its occupation by French forces in 1798. His frank account[37] of their good conduct offended the government, and this was responsible for the failure of earlier attempts to have him promoted.[38] At Killala, Stock was hard-pressed financially.[39] Non-payment of revenue on occasion made it impossible for him to travel. On another occasion he wrote 'My shabby tenant Trench, suspecting me to be in want of money, has sent a proposal about his renewal fine by which I should lose near £200, which I have rejected with disdain'.[40] It is hard to blame him for wishing and, indeed, planning for promotion: in a letter written in January 1810, he expresses hopes of a translation to Killaloe and arranges for a friend to find out its value. On 9 February 1810, he notes that the bishop of Waterford has been promised translation to Elphin and adds 'should the bishop of Elphin die there will be no harm in sending off directly, the letter I left in your hands, to the acting secretary at the castle.' Stock had ten children for whom to provide and since he was the son of a hosier,[41] not like Bishop Trench a scion of the landed aristocracy; he found the prices at his predecessor's auction in Waterford entirely beyond his reach. He remarked somewhat smugly, 'It quite delights me that I have not been tempted to buy furniture unfit for an ecclesiastic.'[42] In spite of all economies, the bishop was forced to admit that 'we shall not sit down in our new situation at less than £1,000. Our comfort may be that whatever we have now, will be very handsome, when at Killala we possessed very little to boast of.'[43] His short episcopate in Waterford and Lismore showed him to be active in the affairs of the diocese even though he was by then 70 years of age and much troubled with gout.[44] When he visited the parishes he was quick to notice things amiss, and his comments could sometimes be rather acid.[45] Dr Stock was not immune from those faults often thought peculiar to his age. Neither he nor his contemporaries saw anything amiss in actions which today would be condemned as nepotism. Writing to his second son, Henry, he says, 'I expect you will not be discontented at my making provision out of my patronage, first for those members of our family who appear to me to stand most in need of it.'[46] His financial affairs were a constant worry,[47] yet he was able to take a country villa near Waterford[48] and in addition he took a house in south Wales for a couple of summers at £100 a year.[49] The bishop, though a scholar, was fully aware of the ways in which patronage was managed:

> Poor Arthur is tempted to wish for interest with Mr John Beresford to suc-
> ceed to the place of postmaster of this office [Waterford] … but wishing
> will not do much. I might as well expect by a wish to succeed to the
> archbishop of Dublin who I understand, is dying of a dropsy on his chest.[50]

The advice which he gave to his children was decidedly practical, not to say wordly.[51] But the reality of the bishop's warm good-nature cannot be denied. He gave 20 guineas towards the provision of the new church at Cappoquin and a similar sum to prevent the schoolhouse at Ardfinnan from falling down,[52] while his concern for the widow of a former employee is very touching.[53] He himself sums up this side of his character: 'I seem to give a good deal yearly to the poor; but God send it may be counted at the last sufficient for my income.'[54] A letter written by the bishop on 9 March 1813 is interesting in itself and also shows that he had a necessary sense of proportion:

> My dame would be glad to have an opportunity of treating some of the barristers with a roasting pig, sent in a basket: pigs here are so far dearer than in Dublin, on account of the Waterford pork-trade, so that we cannot buy a roasting pig of three week for less than a guinea; a price which it would be a sin to pay for it. If you can send the pig you need not let us have ducks. Pretty stuff for me to write!

Just before what was to be his last Christmas, he wrote to Dublin for a supply of bibles and prayer books since 'the dissenters here are striving to take from our Church the merit of distributing bibles and testaments … their activity should stimulate ours.'[55] In his second last letter to his son in Dublin, he cheerfully remarked that 'the effects of the mercurial course grow more perceivable every day in a great freedom from the teasing asthma' and goes on to state that he has arranged his visitation of Waterford diocese for 5 August and that of Lismore diocese for 12 August at Clonmel.[56] Alas he died on 13 August 1813 after an episcopate of only just over three years. There need have been little concern for the welfare of the established church in Ireland had all her chief pastors been of the calibre of Dr Stock.

Bishop Richard Bourke (1813–32) was the son, brother and father of successive earls of Mayo. A graduate of Christ Church, Oxford, he was ordained deacon and priest by his father who was archbishop of Tuam and under whom he held various preferments[57] until his consecration for Waterford in 1813 at the age of 46.[58] The report that he was required to make to the lord lieutenant in 1819 on the state of his dioceses,[59] if not a deliberate attempt at deception, then at least displays a woeful ignorance of even their geography. He claimed that the curate of Mora 'resides at Clonmell the adjoining parish' whereas Mora was in fact an enclave in Cashel diocese about ten miles from Clonmel. He also stated that the distance between Lismore and Tullaghmelan was 'eight or nine miles'; today it is about 17 miles. He claimed that the Revd James Hill curate of Killaloan, Kilcash, Templethay (Temple-Etney?) and Kilgrant 'is resident in an adjoining parish' having stated elsewhere in the report that Hill was resident in Tullaghmelan glebe-house, which is not in any sense an adjoining parish it being about six miles from the western boundary of Killaloan and Kilgrant. He also stated that the Revd William Stephenson vicar of Tullaghorton resides in Clonmel and that 'he also discharges the duties of this parish [Tullaghorton] being only three miles from it'. Tullaghorton is at least 13 miles from Clonmel. It is most unlikely that the bishop was calculating the distances in Irish measurement but even if allowance is made for this, a substantial error still remains in most of the above instances. All this suggests a rather casual acquaintance with his diocese. When, in addition, it is discovered that Bishop Bourke failed to disburse to the builder of Lisronagh church in 1832 funds which had been entrusted to him for that purpose by the board of first fruits, it is clearly impossible to find any cause for enthusiasm about his episcopate. The unfortunate builder, William Tinsley, was informed after the bishop's death that 'there are so many judgment debts on the late bishop's property ... that you have no chance of ever being paid'.[60]

After the death of Bourke, the archbishop of the province, Dr Laurence, succeeded also to Waterford and Lismore under the provisions of the Church Temporalities Act.[61] Although the archbishop was by then 74 years of age, he felt it his duty to remove his place of residence (and consequently that of his successors) to Waterford – a decision which may be questioned for reasons of geography and also because of the desirability of having a prelate of the Irish Church resident in the ecclesiastical capital of Munster. Before his consecration for Cashel in 1822 he had been regius professor of Hebrew at Oxford and a canon of Christ Church.[62] Laurence also had the distinction of being a scholar who continued and indeed extended his studies after his promotion to the bench,[63] which he accepted reluctantly.[64] He is said to have governed his dioceses with ability and tact[65] and he quickly made himself familiar with the problems of the Irish establishment.[66] A comment made about the manner in which he dispensed his patronage is also indicative of the absence of public disapproval of family aggrandizement: 'Arch Bishop Laurence, when he had provided for his two nephews and his son-in-law who were some of the best men ever to have cure of souls, he disposed of his patronage fairly, advancing men in order up the income scale.'[67]

Prior to his consecration for the bishopric of Killaloe in 1836, Dr Stephen Sandes had held no appointments outside Trinity College where he was a fellow and Archbishop King's Lecturer in divinity. He did not share the views of Dr Trench, one of his predecessors at Waterford, on the merits of itinerant preachers for he refused to co–operate in the extension of the archbishop's 'Connaught Home Mission Society' into his diocese of Clonfert.[68] Translated to Cashel, Emly, Waterford and Lismore in 1839, he only enjoyed an episcopate there of three years. Nothing is known of his work in Lismore diocese except that he consecrated the new church of Ardmore on 5 September 1841 and took the opportunity to administer the rite of Confirmation there and in two other parishes in that part of the diocese.[69] Dr Sandes died at his house in Fitzwilliam Square, Dublin on 14 November 1842 in his 64th year[70] and, most appropriately was buried in the chapel of Trinity College.

The name of Bishop Robert Daly (1843–72) became like that of Dr Trench, a household word throughout the Church of Ireland.[71] Of a good family,[72] he had a distinguished university career[73] and in 1807 found himself in holy Orders without having given much thought to his decision.[74] His cousin Eusby Cleaver became archbishop of Dublin 1809 and in that year while still in his first curacy he was given the sinecure prebend of Holy Trinity in Cork cathedral and five years later was appointed to the living of Powerscourt, to which a prebendal stall in St Patrick's was annexed. By now Daly had become a convert to the rising 'low-church' party. A reference which he made to Alexander Knox, the father of the Tractarian movement in Ireland, well illustrates his views: 'I honoured him for his deep tone of personal piety but I feel very thankful that I was delivered from the erroneous doctrines of his school.'[75] He turned Powerscourt into an evangelical centre: Lord and Lady Powerscourt headed his list of 'converts,'[76] he trained young men for the ministry,[77] went on the 'Home Mission'[78] and co-operated with Archbishop Trench of Tuam in his schemes for supplying Irish-speaking clergymen in the west of Ireland.[79] In 1841–2 as the crown nominee for the deanery of St Patrick's, Dublin, he was involved in a disputed election.[80] While the case was still *sub judice* he missed the opportunity of preferment to the more desirable sees of Meath and Ossory.[81] On the same day on which he was installed dean he was offered the bishopric of Cashel by the lord lieutenant, Lord de Grey, and accepted. Lord de Grey was anxious to break the practice by which only supporters of the national system of education were promoted to the bench. Daly was a violent opponent of the national board and his brother had recently been raised to the peerage by the same government.[82]

Bishop Daly was described, probably justly, as 'a man of strong sense, thorough inflexibility of principle and singular honesty of purpose.'[83] The dioceses were not in a very healthy state on his arrival[84] and it was not in his nature to tolerate any laxity or abuse provided he recognized it as such. Many of his acts suggested a despotism – whether one applied the adjective 'benevolent' depended on one's churchmanship. A case in point was that of Revd W.G. Giles, vicar of Dungarvan 1849–54, who adhered strictly to the observance of such holy days as are provided with collect, epistle and gospel in the Prayer Book. Some parishioners took exception to this and refused to attend their parish church. Bishop Daly aided and abetted their schism by providing for worship a house in the parish of Kilrush, an enclave in Dungarvan parish which had been churchless since medieval times 'He carefully excluded from his diocese any clergyman who held Tractarian views'.[85] During his tenure of the see, non-residence of a serious nature underwent a noticeable reduction. Although some of the credit for this must go to new legislation and changing circumstances, the bishop played a very prominent part too. At a visitation of the diocese of Lismore held at Clonmel, Dr Daly called the Revd Francis Cradock, vicar of Whitechurch 'over the coals' for non-residence. A fierce and angry altercation between them lasted for some minutes until at length the bishop 'dropped him'. Cradock turned to an onlooker and said 'the only way is to take him by the muzzle'.[86] During the Famine he was charitable to his people of all denominations[87] while he himself paid for young active curates to old or indifferent incumbents, thus mitigating one of the evils of the establishment, the absence of retiring annuities.[88] However, the manner in which he distributed his patronage did not escape criticism and it was said that 'more than one hundred educated gentlemen and their families were placed to a great extent at his mercy.' In addition he was blamed for giving the living of Templemore in Cashel diocese, worth £700 a year to his godson, a stranger to the diocese, and for appointing to Kilvemnon, of the same value, another stranger, the son of his former clerk and schoolmaster while the Revd George Lawless a curate of 20 years standing was forced to take a military chaplaincy because 'he happened not to have the bishop's shibboleth'.[89]

To many Daly appeared to be 'one of the most narrow-minded, bigoted and intolerant men in the Irish church',[90] while by others more in sympathy with his views he was regarded as 'a busy pastor, a sound preacher and an agreeable platform speaker.'[91] His intolerant and dictatorial manner allied to complete unawareness that the Irish church was anything more than one among several Protestant denominations was much to be regretted yet his hatred of idleness and inefficiency, which was engendered by this very intolerance, left the church stronger in the diocese than possibly ever before.

2. The cathedral church of St Carthagh

The cathedral church of the diocese called after its founder St Carthagh (died 637) dates mainly from a restoration in the 17th century by Richard Boyle, first earl of Cork (1566–1643) having previously been almost destroyed by Edmond Fitzgibbon, the 'White Knight'.[1] Several older features however have survived.[2] A long cruciform building, the addition of a tower and spire[3] and the transformation of the choir into a good specimen of early gothic-revival represent the main structural contributions of the 19th century. In 1746 the Waterford apothecary Charles Smith noted that 'the stalls, seats and galleries are but of a late standing as are the throne and pulpit which are both well carved'. Bishop Gore (d. 1691) had bequeathed £200 towards providing a ring of bells and beautifying the choir. The first direction cannot have been carried out as an illustration shows one bell in a western turret. In 1735 £64 6s. 6d. was laid out for a new throne and pulpit.[4] In 1775 the chapter, having admitted that the cathedral was 'at present out of repair and in a ruinous state', appointed the Revd William Jessop, prebendary of Clashmore, as œconomist, and ordered him to 'contract with skilful persons for the repairs … and from time to time to repair the said cathedral church as necessity may require.'[5] This restoration also resulted in the introduction of an organ, seemingly for the first time: 'Whereas several well-disposed persons have expressed their desire that an organ might be erected … and have offered to subscribe considerable sums towards the building of it', the chapter voted £200 towards the cost of the organ and the repairs and resolved that it should be erected 'over the west door of the choir and that a seat be built for His Grace the Duke of Devonshire in some other part of the gallery'. Thirty-two years later the cathedral was again 'in a most ruinous state' and the chapter resolved that it 'be put into the most beautiful and perfect repair'. Not surprisingly, after this vote of 'no confidence,' Mr Jessop resigned as œconomist and a committee consisting of the dean, the treasurer and the prebendary of Donoughmore and Kiltegan was set up to inspect the repairs.[6] From this restoration dates the present delicate 'Strawberry-hill' decoration of the choir. Unfortunately it both took longer to complete and cost more than the chapter had imagined. By 1811, £300 was due on repairs and salaries and it was decided that work was to continue only until the cathedral was fit for divine service and not to be resumed until the debts were liquidated out of the œconomy fund. The Committee was empowered to borrow not more than £2000 from the board of first fruits while in 1814 a further £1500 was borrowed 'to complete the aisles of the cathedral Church'.[7] Bishop Stock had visited the cathedral in May 1811 and his comments were not complimentary:

> Cathedral – rebuilding at a great expense with a probable lapse of years before it can be completed. Chancel finished with elegance but not large enough to hold the congregation. Disposition of the altar, desk and pulpit as at Stradbally and Killottran, utterly unsuitable to the dignity requisite for the celebration of the Lord's supper, especially in a cathedral church. Divine service performed in the town house, on Sundays only, till the cathedral shall be fit for use.

R.H. Ryland's description of the completed work in 1824 shows that only the choir was furnished and in use:

> Divine service is performed in the place newly fitted up, which taken by itself is a beautiful little church. Over the entrance and beneath a pure Saxon arch, a handsome organ has been erected; the windows are of stained glass richly and exquisitely executed, the work of a native artist George M'Alister of Dublin ... the pulpit and the seats for the chapter are of black oak neatly carved.[8]

By 1827 the debt on the œconomy fund had presumably been paid off for in that year the chapter approved a contract for the erection of a tower and spire and repairs of the aisle at a cost of £3,500 'which has been commenced under the direction of the dean of Lismore'. This suggests that Dean Scott (1796–1828) was the prime mover in this restoration phase. Bishop Stock had commented on the shortage of accommodation in 1811 while in 1837 Dean Cotton also referred to the need to provide for an increasing congregation.[9] This culminated in 1868 in a plan for the destruction of the screen and organ loft 'restoring it to what must have been the original intention of those who have built the church'.[10] As to the latter statement nothing could have been further from the truth and the use of the nave for large congregations and the choir for small does not seem to have been considered.[11] The plan also provided for the removal of 'the unsightly galleries which are at present situated at each side of the chancel' and for the pews, pulpit and stalls 'to be replaced with open benches'.

At Lismore, as at so many other cathedrals, the influence of the bishop had declined in the face of deeply entrenched and resolutely defended interests of the dean and chapter. In this case, two other factors aggravated the position: the residence of the bishops at Waterford, 30 miles from Lismore and the 'peculiar jurisdiction' by which for eleven months of the year, the dean of Lismore exercised ordinary episcopal jurisdiction in the parishes of Lismore, Mocollop and Tallow.[12] In a church that should have been especially his own the role of the bishop was reduced to one of sporadic skirmisher against the peculiar jurisdiction. The limited power of the bishop is revealed by Bishop Trench's attempt to use the œconomy fund and 'by a just appropriation of the dormant fund' restored the cathedral to 'a neat and seemly condition'. In fact when Bishop Trench attempted to control the fund the dean and chapter stated a case to Sir John Nicholl, King's advocate and the bishop submitted the same case to Dr Radcliffe of London and since the opinion of the latter was much stronger in favour of the independence of the dean and chapter, the bishop submitted. Nor could the restoration of the cathedral be amongst the first acts of Bishop Trench. He was consecrated in 1802 and the renovation did not begin until 1807. In 1820 Bishop Bourke demanded proxies and exhibits at his visitation from the dean and chapter as a corporation. They promptly stated a case to Stephen Lushington of Doctors Commons as to whether any deed issuing out of the Bishop's Court at Waterford was admissible within the dean's peculiar jurisdiction. His opinion was that the sending of a writ of sequestration into the jurisdiction of the dean would be equal to sending it into another diocese.[13]

The dean and chapter consisted of five dignitaries and nine prebendaries[14] and was thus one of the largest and most complete in Ireland.[15] All these 14 persons had the rectorial tithes of particular parishes in the diocese appropriated to their several maintenance. The parish or parishes from whom a member of the chapter drew the rectorial tithes was called the *corps* of that member's dignity or prebend. The corps of the deanery was the rectory of Tubrid; the corps of the precentorship, the rectory of Ardmore; the corps of the chancellorship, the rectory of Derrygrath the corps of the treasureship, the rectories of Newcastle and Tullaghmelan; the corps of the archdeaconry, the rectories of Ballybacon, Kilmolash and Kilrush. The corps of each prebend was the rectory of the parish or parishes by whose name the prebend was called. Vicarages had been founded in most of the above parishes and when this was the case, the cure of souls fell to the vicar and not to the dignitary or prebendary who was ex-officio, rector. But in three of the above parishes, called 'entire rectories,' vicarages had not been founded. Thus the treasurer had cure of souls in the parish of Tullaghmelan, the archdeacon had one in the parish of Kilrush and the prebendary of Mora had one in the parish of that name.[16] They also possessed in their corporate capacity, the rectorial tithes of the parish of Lismore and Mocollop. This revenue was called the œconomy fund and was, as has been seen, used to keep the cathedral in repair and to pay its officers and servants.[17] Only three members of the chapter were necessarily *ipso facto* charged with parochial duties – which on the whole they neglected. The duties of the churchless parish of Kilrush were never discharged by the archdeacon in person nor was the tiny churchless parish of Mora ever served by the prebendary in person. When Dr Charles Tuckey became treasurer in 1804, he continued to hold his benefice of Shanrahan by faculty and employed a curate for Tullaghmelan. His successor, Treasurer Perry was resident in Tullaghmelan glebe-house.[18] It does not follow that the remaining 11 canons were resident, either simultaneously or in rotation at Lismore. The incomes of four did not amount to a 'living wage' or to say the same thing in 19th-century terms, were 'on a value too small to afford comfort to the incumbent',[19] but there was no adequate reason why the remaining seven canons should not have made their homes at Lismore for at least part of the year. The dean, Sir George Bishopp, who was also archdeacon of Aghadoe, with cure of souls, had a house in Baggot Street, Dublin,[20] and enjoyed a combined income of £1,500 a year.[21] Of the remainder, the precentor and the prebendary of Disert and Kilmoleran held benefice in other dioceses and were resident on them. The precentor, a brother of Bishop Bourke, held two benefices; Ardfinnan in the diocese of Lismore and Kilmacow in the diocese of Ossory. He kept a curate in Ardfinnan glebe-house and himself discharged the duties of Kilmacow. His three appointments brought him a combined income of £921 a year. The prebendary of Disert and Kilmoleran, Nicholas Herbert, was resident on his benefice of Knockgraffon in Cashel diocese enjoying a net combined income of £1,118 *per annum*.[22] The prebendary of Donoughmore and Kiltegan was vicar of his prebendal parish and was resident in the glebe house;[23] the prebendary of Kilgobinet was an assistant chaplain in Dublin,[24] and the remaining two prebendaries – Tullaghorton and Kilrossanty – seem to have been without other clerical work.[25] The prebendary of Tullaghorton, Henry Pretty Perry, had been vicar of Derrygrath 1822–30 worth about £80 a years, (his family home, Woodroofe, was in the parish). In the latter year he married a daughter of Bishop Bourke and was appointed by him to this prebend worth £237 net a year. In 1834 he became Treasurer. At this time the duty of the dean was 'to govern the cathedral and its members and to officiate therein'.[26] The other dignitaries denied having any duties whatever while those of the prebendaries were returned as preaching occasionally in the cathedral church and attending chapter meetings'.[27] Under the Act 4 & 5 William IV cap. 90 most of the dignities and prebends were suspended[28] and their incomes transferred to the Ecclesiastical Commissioners. At disestablishment (1869) only the deanery, the treasureship, the archdeaconry and the prebends of Disert and Kilmoleran, Kilrossanty and Clashmore remained, while the precentorship, the chancellorship and the prebend of Modeligo had been restored by the chapter as unendowed posts.[29] The archdeacon was the only member of the chapter resident and the idea of using a stall as a mark of dignity for parish clergymen was now becoming established, for all the dignitaries except the dean and three out of four prebendaries were beneficed within the four united dioceses.[30] Yet despite this record of neglect of duty, particularly in the first half of the century, it is an inescapable if unpalatable truth that the members of chapters in the 19th century had a much closer connection with their cathedral than their successors today who have come to regard the prefix 'canon' – never used in the 19th century – as merely a title of honour bestowed on them after long service in the ministry. Dean Scott (1796–1828) and Dean Cotton (1834–49) made the effort to find houses near the cathedral and it is not surprising that these were the only two deans to leave any material impression. Scott was leader of the restoration early in the century and in the erection of the tower and spire just before his death. Henry Cotton was possibly the finest dean in the history of Saint Carthagh's. He had been sub-librarian of the Bodleian before coming to Ireland in 1823 as domestic chaplain to his father-in-law, Archbishop Laurence. In 1834 the chapter elected him 'to the honourable but unremunerative dignity of dean of Lismore' and despite the fact that he continued to hold two benefices in Cashel diocese he came to live at Lismore, and officiated regularly in the cathedral whose welfare he made his particular concern. He made every effort to make the vicars choral effective and was instrumental, in 1840, in preventing the suppression of their corporation which had been ordered by the Ecclesiastical Commissioners. In 1845 he founded the Diocesan Library of Lismore and from his own contributions and those of his personal friends in Ireland and England more than 2,000 volumes were obtained. They may still be seen in the room attached to the cathedral that the chapter erected for them. Although he ceased to be dean when the suspension was removed in 1849, he seems to have at least retained his house at Lismore where he died in 1879. A distinguished scholar with many publications, his monumental *Fasti Ecclesiae Hibernicae* is still in use today.[31] A house was built at Lismore, about 1795, for the archdeacon[32] and probably from that date (and certainly from 1810)[33] the archdeacon was generally resident, although throughout the period he was also a vicar choral. In addition a prebendary was also resident at Lismore for a considerable portion of the period under the guise of headmaster of the diocesan school or curate to the vicars.[34]

The vicars choral were first instituted by Bishop Griffin Christopher (1223–46) and in their corporate capacity had cure of souls in the parish of Lismore and Mocollop – a very large area.[35] The great problem regarding this corporation in the 19th century was the apparent impossibility of securing the residence of all five simultaneously on an income little more and sometimes less than that of a curate. In 1831 and the two previous years the average income of the corporation was £746 which after payment of a curate for Lismore and another for Mocollop and also a schoolmaster left each vicar with £115. In 1837 the income of the corporation was £720 but in 1840–1 each vicar only received about £73.[36] In 1807 Bishop Trench stated that one of the vicars always reside at Lismore and perform the duty for which he was paid £50 by the corporation.[37] Yet this disguises the fact that two other vicars, Lovett and Sullivan were resident at Lismore and probably also a fourth, Ryan.[38] In 1836 only the archdeacon, the curate and the preacher were returned as resident[39] and of these only Archdeacon Power was a vicar choral. Sullivan had now retired as preacher on a pension of £65 a year,[40] but he was still a vicar-choral and living at Lismore.[41] On 29 April 1837 the ecclesiastical commissioners recommended the suppression of the corporation of vicars choral under the provisions of 6 and 7 William IV cap. 99.[42] Dean Cotton immediately sprang to their defence. He admitted that of late years the duties had been performed by curates and a portion of the expense improperly thrown on the œconomy fund, but he argued that he had plans in hand to make the vicars effective by placing one vicar at Mocollop where there was a church and school, another at Cappoquin which also by now had its church and school, two to do the heavy duty at Lismore and to use the income of the remaining vicar choralship to pay choirmen and boys.[43] He asked, 'if a duty has been inefficiently done surely the best way is to cause it to be fully performed, not to prevent for ever the performance which is actually required'.[44] Dr Cotton held that the corporation was improving every year. Three vicars were resident and the other two would be placed at Mocollop and Cappoquin as soon as the absentees resigned. Cotton's intervention was happily successful: the vicars appealed to the privy council and their rights were re-established on 29 April 1840.[45] His plans came nearest to fruition in the years 1841–5. Four vicars officiated in their cathedral church[46] – one of them was curate of Mocollop – and only one was absent. But one, Mockler, disappeared in 1845; another, Butler, became chaplain of Villierstown in 1847. Samuel Meyrick came in that year as vicar and curate at Lismore and three vicars regularly officiated until 1850. But Richard Woods became vicar of Lisgenan and ceased to officiate at Lismore after 1851 and only Power and Meyrick remained. The exodus of vicars and the reason was described in mock Chaucerian lines in a work – *Ye Fyve Clerkes of Lysmore*, author unknown, date about 1850 among manuscripts of the dean of Lismore. The margins are filled with amusing line drawings to illustrate the text:

Once upon a tyme five Clerkes there were,
  Goode men, I weene, and true;
Theyre dutyes, well, all through ye yeare
  Right able for to do.

And from an old Cathedraff Church
  A pencion fayre they had
Full fyftye poundes a yeare to each
  Theyre hearts to make glad.

These Clerkes were Vicayres Chorall hight
  There dutye was to syng,
In Romish tymes ye daylye Mass,
  There ancient Church within.

But Protestantys doe not lyke
  Those daylye services,
Soe Clerkes came to spend theyre tyme
  Allmost in ydlenesse.

Soe, deeming two would be ynuff
  To take care of theyre Church.
They sayd that three, to eke theyre meanes,
  For other worke might search.

Ye worke they sought, in tyme they found
  One got a Chaplainage,
And one dyd get a Vycarage
  And one a Rectorye.

While of ye two that stayed at home
  One was Archdeacon made,
And t'other got some lyttel things
  Which fayrelye well hym payd.

And all ye five respected were,
  For they could paye theyr waye,
And charitable actes agreed
  With what men heard them saye,

And fyftye pounds was not ynuff,
  For any of ye five;
For yf a Clerk have Wyfe or Chylde
  'Twill hardlye keepe alive.

Thus all Cotton's plans collapsed after he had ceased to be dean in 1849.[47]
  Meyrick left Lismore in 1861 to become incumbent of Blessington in the diocese of Glendalough,[48] and at disestablishment only one vicar, Archdeacon Power, remained in residence.[49] It has been recently suggested that 'despite its college of vicars, Lismore was the most flagrant and notorious instance of the cathedral service and system having fallen into disuse. The parochial duties alone were recognised and the bad custom arose of the college appointing a deputy or curate – sometimes from its own body – to attend to them'.[50] While admitting the truth of most of this, it must be remembered that considering the size of the parish, the cure of souls was the vicar's heaviest responsibility and provision was always made for its discharge. The rota of services in the cathedral church was really exemplary for the period: there was divine service twice on Sundays and once on Wednesdays, Fridays and 'every holiday' and the Eucharist was celebrated monthly.[51] It was through the action of a vicar choral that an organ was obtained in 1775 and an organist appointed.[52] During the restoration of

1807 the chapter 'expected that Mr Stanistreet (the organist) continue to instruct the children in singing.'[53] In about 1834 there was an organist and seven boy choristers though admittedly they were maintained out of the œconomy fund.[54] As has been seen, it was only during the last years of the period that the number of resident vicars-choral dropped to one while for the first 22 years of the century four vicars were resident.

If under the establishment the cathedral corporations 'were too frequently mere nests of jobbery and scandalous misappropriation of funds'[55] it gave an infinitely better basis for improvement than the position of the cathedral church today. No vicars have been appointed since disestablishment. Only the dean is resident but in popular thought he is little more than incumbent of the parish.

2. The south prospect of the cathedral church of St Carthagh in Lismore

3. The parishes, their boundaries, and incomes

The diocese of Lismore is divided into 74 parishes, many of which are, however, very small and have been for centuries without church or resident priest. They are amongst the most ancient of Irish territorial divisions being based on the pre-invasion *tuatha* and *triocha céad*. The more recent churches, erected between the 12th and 16th centuries, were mostly destroyed or allowed to fall into disrepair in the post-Reformation period.[1] The established church continued to treat these numerous parishes as the basis of her organisation but following medieval practice, combined a number of contiguous parishes under the same parish priest either in plurality for the lifetime of a particular incumbent, or by permanent union.[2] Sometimes parishes were cut off from the main body of the diocese or portions of a parish might exist as an enclave in another. Kilworth parish was at one time part of Lismore diocese although surrounded by Cloyne; a portion of Lismore was isolated in Cashel diocese and was itself divided between two parishes – Mora and Inishlounaght; three small portions of Clonea parish were scattered in that of Dungarvan which was itself divided into three portions by the estuary of the river Colligan and the parish of Kilrush; most of Ardmore parish was six to 10 miles from the parish church and only connected with it by a narrow corridor through the Drum hills and a further fragment of this parish was situated five miles in an opposite direction, two other parishes intervening. This fragmentation of parishes had arisen in order to include separated tribal or family lands within the local unit of organization.[3] At disestablishment all these portions were included in the parishes that surrounded them, but before, although their inhabitants naturally attended the nearest church they were, strictly speaking, under the charge of a far-distant clergyman and before the commutation of tithe had to contribute to his support. The parochial system was probably introduced as a result of the Anglo-Norman conquest.[4] The rector of a parish might be a cleric, a layman or a corporation such as a monastery and if for any reason the rector was prevented from undertaking the care of the parish, then a vicarage might be founded and endowed usually with one-third of the tithes of the parish, the other two-thirds falling to the rector.[5] It is important to remember that the word vicar did not correspond to our modern use of the word curate. He had cure of souls and the parson's freehold and would employ a curate if non-resident.[6] Non-residence was perhaps the most glaring abuse in the church in the 19th century. It was, however, often a product more of the cramping fetters of the establishment than a manifestation of culpable neglect among individuals. The division of parishes into rectories and vicarages resulted in an inadequate income for the priest to whom the cure of souls was committed. The organization of Derrygrath parish in the early 19th century gives a picture in minature of the confusion caused by appropriation and non-residence. John Cleland was chancellor of St Carthagh's and therefore rector of Derrygrath, without cure of souls 1796–1834. The vicars choral had been founded as early as the 13th century to supply the place of canons absent from the cathedral, presumably because of their parochial duties. But the chancellor was absent both from cathedral and parish and the vicar of Derrygrath was also non-resident in the parish and one of the vicars choral of the cathedral at least 18 miles from Derrygrath. A further irony was that the vicar of Derrygrath was acting as deputy for the other vicars choral. Bishop Trench realizing that the vicars' income of 'under £160' was inadequate to secure a resident clergyman, recommended in 1807 that the rectorial tithe of £123 should be united to the vicarage. Cleland was also precentor of Ardmagh and received £1,415 net per annum from the parish which formed the corps of that dignity. The sum that he received for doing precisely nothing in Lismore diocese was of little significance to him but yet would have been sufficient to secure a resident incumbent for Derrygrath. In 1837 the vicar was living in Clonmel for lack of a house in the parish.[7] While the siphoning-off of tithes into lay hands is a feature of the pre-disestablishment church which is little short of scandalous, at least to present day opinion, arguments could be, and were, put forward to justify the maintenance of the parson of a particular parish by all the inhabitants of that parish, irrespective of their denominational allegiance. But it was clearly unreasonable to expect people – the great majority of them Roman Catholics – to pay the greater portion of their tithe to an absentee layman and the remainder to an absentee clergyman. In only 12 parishes in the diocese in 1837 did the rectorial as well as the vicarial tithes fall to the person to whom cure of souls was committed.[8] The rectorial tithes of 17 parishes[9] amounting to some £4,608 a year were in the possession of the duke of Devonshire, the successor of the Elizabethan adventurer whose aggrandizements Strafford had tried in vain to stop. The rectorial tithes of a further 15 parishes[10] were attached to dignities or prebends in the cathedral church and the remainder were in private possession.

A comparison between a return of *c.*1766[11] and that made by Bishop Trench in 1807[12] shows the changes in parish groupings within that period. In the earlier return 21 groups are given while in 1807, exclusive of dignities and prebends without cure of souls attached, there were 30 benefices. However, the increase is more apparent than real. The return of 1766 gives a system of groupings based not on the theoretical and legal position but on the actual practice followed which in several cases conflicted with the legal position. Donoughmore and Kiltegan, Inishlounaght and Kilronan were held in 1766 to form a union with Clonmel. Strictly speaking all were separate benefices. The rector of Clonmel, Joseph Moore, was also curate to the rector of Inishlounaght and the vicar of Donoughmore and Kiltegan, both non-resident, while the curate to the absent vicar of Kilronan was another Moore, possibly Joseph's son. The only real changes in the parishes between 1766 and 1806 were the building of a church in 1780 for the entire rectory of Tullaghmelan[13] and the separation of Stradbally from Mothel in 1791 prior to the erection of the church. Besides recommending the consolidation of rectory and vicarage in many parishes, Dr Trench drew up a careful scheme for more convenient unions and for the building of churches. He suggested that churches should be built at Clashmore, Derrygrath, Kilgobinet, Kinsalebeg, Dunhill, Kilwatermoy, Garrangibbon, Newtownlennan and Killaloan and hoped to make possible these new centres of church life by perpetually uniting to them neighbouring parishes where churches were not required. He introduced a new idea as regards plurality. Hitherto, and indeed for many years after, unions were too often created to provide a handsome income for an individual with little thought for the efficient discharge of the spiritual duties. Thus from 1786 Kilronan parish was episcopally united to Whitechurch for the benefit of the Revd Thomas Sandiford despite the fact that they were separated by many miles of desolate hill country. Newtownlennan was episcopally united to Clonegam for successive incumbents between 1754 and 1867. Newtownlennan had no church and was at least five miles from that of Clonegan. Monksland was, prior to the suppression, a dependency of the abbey of Inishlounaght and continued to be held with Inishlounaght parish, though separated from it by a vast extent of country, until 1867.[14] New churches were eventually placed where suggested by Bishop Trench except in the case of Kilgobinet, Garrangibbon and Newtownlennan. It is an ironic fact that of the six churches recommended by him in 1806 and eventually built, all except Dunhill and Kilwatermoy are today no longer in use.

In 1818 a report similar to that of 1807 was made by the archbishops and bishops of Ireland.[15] The diocese of Lismore now had 39 benefices and 24 churches in repair.[16] This represented an increase of nine benefices since 1807, but only three churches. Thus there were now 15 churchless benefices as opposed to 12 in 1807. Instead of being removed, the abuse had in the space of 13 years been aggravated further. However, in three of the churchless benefices, the building of churches was already in hand.[17] The three new churchless benefices were Kilmolash, Mortlestown and Newcastle (Co. Tipperary). Kilmolash 'a small parish under £100' and Newcastle 'under the value of £200' were being used to subsidize curates but the occupation, if any, of the rector of Mortlestown ('under £200') is not recorded.[18] Bishop Bourke must have been either a knave or a fool to add 'no residence yet'[19] for the parish was of diminutive extent and the erection of church or glebe-house was never seriously considered. The motive for the erection of these sinecure benefices is not hard to imagine. Put crudely it was thus: 'Why should not parishes be taken away from wealthy benefices and erected into separate benefices? Why should not impecunious curates and deserving friends have a fairer share of the loaves and fishes of church preferment?' As far as it went, it was an estimable doctrine but it completely ignored the principle that the cure of souls was primarily intended for the sanctification of the people of God and only secondarily for the adequate support of the clerical profession. By 1835 there were 41 benefices with cure of souls, the highest number during our period. This represented an increase of two from 1819 while the number of churches was now 31, an increase of seven.[20] The two new single-parish benefices were Colligan and Kilronan but, as neither had a church and the incumbents were non-resident, the change must have made little impact on the parishioners.[21]

In 1867, at the end of the period the number of benefices was still 41, but this concealed the fact that important changes had taken place in their arrangement.[22] Eight new benefices appeared and the same number were suppressed. Cappoquin and Mocollop were by now legally separated from the parish of Lismore. Templetenny had been removed from Shanrahan union and its church (built in 1827) and resident incumbent were placed in the substantial village of Ballyporeen. The other new benefices were Guilcagh, Lisgenan, Newtownlennan, Templemichael (Co. Tipperary) and Killaloan. The last named had in theory been separated from Kilcash but it was in fact much the stronger of the two and it alone had a church.[23] Guilcagh was separated from Dunhill in 1850 and its new church consecrated early in the following year but the remaining three benefices represented a revival of the bad old system of using the revenues of a churchless benefice for the support of a priest who may, or may not, have been doing useful work elsewhere. In 1861 the three benefices had a combined church population of only 20 people.[24] The suppression[25] of the entire rectories of Donoughmore and Mora and the vicarages of Kilbarrymeaden, Kilmolash, Modeligo, Newcastle (Co. Tipperary), Seskinan and Tullaghorton was long overdue. None of these benefices had churches nor were they likely to need them in the foreseeable future.

Clerical incomes in the diocese and throughout the Church of Ireland, seem, allowing for the change in the value of money, to have been at a much higher level in the 19th century than they are today. They could also fluctuate between much wider limits and it is not really possible to arrive at an average stipend to which the majority of income approximated more of less closely. In the 18th century incomes appear small to modern eyes. Of those parishes with churches, the three town parishes of Clonmel, Dungarvan and Tallow came first with £132, £120 and £110 respectively.[26] Ardmore, Tubrid and Whitechurch were each worth £40 *per annum*.[27] Ardfinnan was the poorest with £15 a year[28] but it must not be imagined that the vicar, William Downes, was penniless – he was also chancellor of St Carthagh's at £60 a year,[29] vicar of the neighbouring churchless parish of Newcastle at 'about twenty or twenty-five pounds'[30] and was curate of Cahir and Mortlestown.[31] In the report of 1807 Bishop Trench was asked to note those benefices whose incomes were 'of a value too small to afford comfort to the incumbent'.[32] He gives eight livings under this head[33] – none of the above were among them – and gives their incomes, none of which were above £160. Thus it can be assumed that the remaining benefices were above that figure and, in the opinion of the bishop, of sufficient value. The same question was asked in the report of 1819[34] and Bishop Bourke also gives eight benefices as too poor[35] – none of them were worth more than £200.

The report of 1837 gives a comprehensive picture of parish incomes.[36] Clonmel, Dungarvan and Tallow worth £132, £120 and £110 respectively in 1746 now yielded to £657, £555 and £370. The country parishes of Ardmore, Ardfinnan, Tubrid and Whitechurch were worth respectively £254, £172, £377 and £189. The salary of a curate is a useful guide to the minimum living wage possible for a clergyman and when it is realized that at this time most of the curates were getting £75 a year – some of them were married – it can be seen that, in comparison, incumbents were quite well off.[37] The incomes of benefices shown in the report of 1867–8[38] are of special interest as the tithes were by then commuted into a rent charge of 75% of their former nominal value. A definite if not very drastic reduction of income was the result. Clonmel was now worth £623 a year; Dungarvan had fallen to £502; Whitechurch with the addition of Colligan (worth £42 in 1837) was reduced by only £5. The royal commissioners fixed as their ideal income, one of £300 a year after the payment of all expenses including that of a curate.[39] Only eight benefices in Lismore diocese filled this requirement. The average income in Lismore was only £211 but this was very close to the national average – £210.[40] The level of incumbents' incomes in the neighbouring diocese of Cashel was well above average – £344.

Much controversy in the pre-disestablishment period centred round the population figures and in particular the census returns for 1831 and 1861. It was pointed out that in the earlier census the Methodists had been included with the members of the established church, but dealt with separately in 1861 and it was held that the church of Ireland had not lost ground in the country.[41] This seems to have been substantially true as far as the diocese of

Lismore was concerned. In 1831 the total population was 186,265[42] and in 1861, it was 145,396.[43] The 'Protestant population' in 1836 was 5,579[44] and yet in 1861 the 'church population' was 4,775.[45] It was in the matter of benefices that Lismore diocese was most vulnerable to hostile attack. There were 11 benefices with less than 20 members of the established church, and this was the highest number in any diocese in Ireland with one exception.[46]

It is clear that many of the absurdities of parochial organisation to which reference has been made in this chapter were due to the fact that 'society' outgrows the forms and dimensions in which its provision for religious ministration and superintendence was originally cast. In this way many instances of endowment unsuitable to the circumstances of the locality – large when the congregation is small and small when it is large – have arisen.'[47] It should also be remembered that 'great irregularities and anomalies in the distribution of church revenue, relatively to area and population existed both in England and Ireland at a period long anterior to the Reformation.'[48] Yet it is difficult to avoid the conclusion that insufficient energy was shown by the bishops in the suppression of small, and the division of large, benefices, for which they were provided with ample powers.[49] The system of patronage was probably responsible, for although the consent of the patrons was not a pre-requisite to alterations in the arrangement of benefices, it was unlikely that the bishop could succeed against powerful family influence even should he be prepared to make the attempt.[50]

4. Incumbents and curates

A very great change has taken place in the character of the clergy of the diocese in the space of 150 years. An inescapable and welcome feature of the pre-disestablishment church was the presence of the aristocracy and gentry in the ranks of the clergy. As their numbers noticeably declined after 1869 and are non-existent today, it is difficult to avoid the conclusion that they were enticed into the sacred ministry by the expectation of a rapid rise to the better-endowed posts.[1] Apart from the more spectacular cases of pluralism and non-residence, the parochial clergy were, on the whole, a band of quiet country gentlemen attentive to their not very arduous duties,[2] which might be summarized as to exert a general benevolent influence over the people committed to their charge, to visit the sick and afflicted and conduct the services of the church. Throughout Ireland at this time the usual order of public worship was 'the celebration of divine service once, and in many cases twice, on all Sundays, but more generally, in most of the country churches, twice in summer and once in winter ... The Sacrament of the holy communion is duly administered in all the churches at certain stated periods and a catechetical examination of the children is, for the most part held weekly.'[3] The parishes of the diocese did not, on the whole, fall below or much exceed the national average in this respect. The return of Ringagosnagh in 1836 may be taken as typical of the country churches: 'Sacrament administered four times in the year, divine service once every Sunday, Good Friday and Christmas Day.' Clonegam, Mothel and Whitechurch only had the sacrament at Easter, Whitesuntide and Christmas. Inishlounaght, Killaloan and Tullaghmelan had it six times a year. Affane and Lisronagh had it every second month and at the principal festivals, Ardfinnan was eight times a year.[4] Most of the town and a few of the country churches had monthly celebrations. Cahir, Cappoquin, Carrick, Clonmel, Kinsalebeg Shanrahan, Tallow, Templemichael and Villierstown had a monthly celebration, while Clonmel had two celebrations at Christmas and Easter. Ardfinnan, Cahir, Shanrahan, Tubrid and Villierstown had divine service twice on Sundays. Carrick excelled with three services every Sunday while Shanrahan was the only church with a service on week-days. Yet the parliamentary returns for the same period state that there was service on all Wednesdays and Fridays in Dungarvan and Clonmel, on all Fridays in Tallow and on Wednesdays and Fridays during Lent in Carrick.[5]

If a man was fortunate enough to secure a comfortable living in his youth, there he was usually content to stay, quite unaffected by such modern crazes as a desire for thorough training as a curate, a strenuous parish in the prime of life with perhaps lighter work and then retirement in old age. Henry Palmer, son of the archdeacon of Ossory and precentor of St Carthagh's, was educated by Bishop Stock then rector of Delgany and in 1805 married his daughter, Maria.[6] When Stock was translated to Waterford and Lismore in 1810 he gave the living of Tubrid and Ballybacon to his son-in-law. Palmer remained vicar there for 54 years and on his death was succeeded by his son who reigned at Tubrid for a further 22 years until he did in 1886.[7] About 1831 the net annual income of the benefice was £550 – one of the best in the diocese[8] and the church population of Tubrid was only 115.[9] By 1868 the net income had dropped to £400 but the church population was now only 29.[10] Dr John Devereus, vicar of Stradbally 1799–1836, was visited in 1811 by Bishop Stock whose description of the visit effectively portrays the pleasant and easy lives of many country clergymen in the 19th century:

> Union of three parishes contains but nine Protestant families. Children catechised about 14. Incumbent often obliged to leave the parish, requires a curate. Rector and curate live in contiguous houses ... Dr Dix a widower without family, easy in circumstances, the living being worth £700 or £800 p.a. very hospitable. All well here.[11]

Ambrose Power, archdeacon of Lismore for 40 years (1828–68) was during this time probably the most prominent clergyman in the diocese. His father was created a baronet in 1836 and his mother was the daughter of an MP and niece of Henry Grattan.[12] The archdeacon was resident at Lismore in what was technically his glebe-house and he also had a villa at Ardmore, 'the Brighton of Ireland'.[13] At the time of his appointment his net annual income was £579 together with £115 from his vicar choralship.[14] He inherited an estate at Barrettstown, Co. Tipperary, and other lands, from a cousin[15] and was able to take his place in county society into which his children married.[16] This demonstrates not only the aristocratic nature of the archdeacon's position but also the facility shown by him and his family in becoming integrated into local society, a quality which is noticeably absent in the clergy of the present day. With a parochial clergy closely connected with a particular locality by family and land connections, such as those of the archdeacon, very long incumbencies were likely to be the result.[17] Mr Power seems to have at least acquiesced in Bishop Daly's evangelical regime for he attended the bishop's monthly clerical meetings at Waterford and 'brought over some of the Lismore clergy in a drag'.[18]

A notable family ministry was that of the Herberts of Carrick. Nicholas Herbert, vicar of Carrick, Kilmurry and Kilsheelan 1760–1803, was son of Edward Herbert, MP of Muckross, Co. Kerry.[19] His daughter has left a very frank account of his youth and the severely practical motives for his taking holy orders:

> He was noted throughout the County for Boyish Archness and went by the Name of Wild Nick – When he grew up, he studied Physick for a time – but his relation Lord Powis offering him the living of Ludlow, he got into Orders, and lived many years at Ludlow, a Batchelor very much beloved and a great favourite at Powis Castle – Those he deemed amongst the happiest Days of his Life – but a better Preferment being offer'd to my Grandfather for him, he brought his Son over to Ireland to take possession of the United livings of Carrick, Kilmurry and Kilsheelan, and also of the Parish of Knockgrafton under the Patronage of the Butler Family now Lord Ormond.[20]

Nicholas Herbert married a daughter of the first Lord Desart (a Co. Kilkenny family) and they settled down to rear nine children in their 'beautiful little villa near Carrick on Suir',[21] which notwithstanding possessed seven large bedrooms.[22] There their life was pleasantly occupied in visits to their neighbours – among the more important were Lord and Lady Tyrone[23] and 'Old Arch Bishop Cox' of Castletown.[24] Then, as now, a bishopric was regarded as the goal of clerical ambition. In 1776 the Herbert family made a three months expedition to England. Leaving his wife and children at 'Bristol hotwells' Mr Herbert went in search of promotion:

> He went up to London to visit Lord Powis his former Pupil – Lord Powis received him kindly but being in Opposition had No Power to serve him in an application for a Bishopric which was then in Contemplation but which failed by the Supiness of My Father's Friends.[25]

Archbishop Cox's successor, Charles Agar, disrupted the pleasant life somewhat. In 1788 Mr Herbert was compelled to lay out £1,000 on building a new Glebe House at Knockgraffon within five miles of Cashel and 20 miles from Carrick which being now just completed the bishop compelled him to reside there three months in every year.[26] His son Otway became his curate at Carrick in 1791 and only three years later, secured a living in the most singular circumstances:

> The County Kilkenny Militia has been station'd in Carrick for some time – Their Officers were mostly all related to us – By their coming Mrs Rothe got her husband and Otway a good Living – Lord Ormond was my Father's Patron – Otway gave him and his Regiment a grand Dinner here from which the Ladies were excluded – His Lordship took such a liking to my Brother that he could do nothing

without him and to testify his Regard he transfer'd the Living of Knockgraffon from my Father to Otway which, as my Brother was very Young appeared a most Advantageous Renewal.

Otway Herbert seems to have been given to behaviour even then unusual in a clergyman. Two years after he had become rector of Knockgraffon he eloped with a young lady of only 16 years who had been educated in a convent and 'They got themselves married on the Road and were re-married by license in Dublin'. When in the summer of 1797 rebellion broke out in the neighbourhood Otway, characteristically, 'though a clergyman volunteer'd to fight'. In the following year his tithe proctor was hacked to pieces with his wife at Knockgraffon parsonage. Herbert's bed was 'pierced in a hundred places to show what they would have done had he been there'.[27] In 1800 Otway Herbert died from the effects of a fall out hunting and in 1803 his father also died. The epitaph of this estimable 18th-century parson was written by his daughter who incidentally reveals the principles underlying the bestowal of patronage:

> At his Decease the three livings went back to the Patron Lord Ormond and were purchased by Mr Grady and Mr Lloyd of the County of Limerick – Thus upward of eighteen hundred a Year went out of the Family after an Incumbency of forty Years – The whole time he lived Adored and Respected in his parishes and hardly ever quitted them for a Moment – indeed I believe the Parishioners felt all due Gratitude and Regret for him and his son.[28]

The Herbert dynasty was not however at an end. On the contrary it survived even the church establishment: 'We had now but one small Stake left in the beloved Church and that was my Brother Nick who as soon as he was able after the severe Stroke, set off to get himself ordain'd'. The new vicar, Standish Grady, gave him the curacy of Carrick, and in 1810 he secured the sinecure prebend of Disert and Kilmoleran (across the river from Carrick) which he held until his death in 1875 at the age of 92.[29] He was vicar of Drumlease, in the diocese of Kilmore, 1811–24[30] and rector of Knockgraffon, the parish formerly held by his father and brother, from 1824 until 1863.[31] His combined net annual income about 1831 was £1,118.[32]

Another long incumbency was that of Thomas Stanley Monck, rector of Clonegam and vicar of Newtownlennan, 1802–42,[33] who probably owed his preferment to family connections with the Beresfords.[34] He had two sons also in holy orders and one of them, George Stanley came to him as curate in 1825.[35] About 1831 the net annual income of the living, after expenses including £42 as house-rent, was £460 although the curate's salary of £80 must be subtracted from this.[36] After his son became curate, the name of the rector only appeared once in the parish register and he died in 1842 aged 80. His successor under whom George Stanley Monck was continued as curate fortunately only stayed a year being advanced to a more lucrative position in the diocese of Meath.[37] An entry in the register testifies to a resumption of the Monck dynasty:

> 1843 April 30th Revd Geo. Stanley Monck A.M. Curate of this parish since the 18th of October 1825 five was this day inducted as Rector by Revd Usher Lee, Dean of Waterford. Geo. Stanley Monck, Rector.

He held the living until 1867 and thus ended with the church establishment a family ministry of more than 60 years. Two entries in the parish register in 1835, in Monck's own handwriting, show that although the clerical profession may not have been very laborious, it's members did not escape those tragedies common to all: 'Nov 17th Baptized Maria daughter of Revd Geo. Stanley Monck & Susan his wife of Coolfin by Geo. Stanley Monck, Curate'. The next entry is 'Nov 22nd Buried Maria daughter of Revd Geo. Stanley Monck by Geo. Stanley Monck, Curate.'

At no time during the period did the number of churches in the diocese equal the number of benefices and when an incumbent found himself without a church, the natural result was that he absented himself altogether from the benefice. There were however incumbents who were absent from benefices possessed of an adequate income, church, glebe-house and Protestant population and it is difficult to excuse the bishop who did not strain every resource in the prosecution of these unfaithful priests. In 1806 there were 31 benefices but only 19 churches with a further two in process of building.[38] The incumbents of the 10 churchless benefices were all non-resident. Of these, three were engaged in other work within the diocese and were responsible in person for the duties of their benefices, two others were still within the diocese but their benefices were looked after by neighbouring clergymen; one was living on his other benefice in the diocese of Waterford; three were living outside the diocese (Archdeacon Smith on his benefice in Dublin & Mr Stokes of Outeragh on his benefice of Carnalway in the diocese of Kildare). The remaining churchless benefice (Lisronagh) was vacant.[39] When it is discovered that 12 of the 18 incumbents whose benefices had churches, were non-resident, something of the magnitude of the problem can be realised. Three lived near enough to do the duty in person; two lived in the city of Waterford, Draper of Tubrid as surrogate and Flewry of Inishlounaght as archdeacon and rector of St Patrick's; three were vicars-choral at Lismore; four were absent altogether from the united diocese, two definitely living on other benefices.[40] Considering that 22 out of 31 beneficed clergymen were in some sense non-resident, it is surprising to find Bishop Trench observing at the end of his report, 'I have never experienced any difficulty in obtaining the residence of the clergy.'[41] But of course in all cases of non-residence it must be remembered that the parochial duties were discharge by curates, usually resident.

Bishop Bourke's report in 1819[42] shows a slight improvement – 25 of the 39 clergymen with cure of souls, were non-resident. Seven were living near their benefices and performing the duties in person; three were again vicars-choral at Lismore; five were employed on other work within the diocese; one was surrogate at Waterford and therefore exempt from residence by 48 George III cap. 66 and two others were beneficed in Waterford diocese; seven were living outside the diocese and this represents an increase of three on the figure for 1806. The report of 1837 shows that of the 41 benefices, 13 were still without churches.[43] In all 22 priests were non-resident on their benefices. Six pleaded difficulty in obtaining houses within their parishes and lived near enough to do the duty in person; three were engaged in other clerical work within the diocese; two were on the staff of the cathedral church; two were on other benefices in the diocese of Waterford; three were 'resident in the city of Waterford' and one was a curate there; six were altogether absent from the dioceses. The extent of non-residence in the final phase of the establishment can be deduced from returns ordered in 1863 and 1864.[44] The number of benefices is given as 41 in both reports but there is a discrepancy for the number of non-resident incumbents. Fifteen are so recorded in the earlier report but 19 in the later one. The details in the second report are fuller and since the return of 1863 was rather ominously directed solely at the united diocese, there would be a natural desire to present as favourable an impression as possible. There had also been a change of registrar. Nineteen non-resident out of 42 incumbents was the lowest figure during our period and since nine of these were able to discharge their duties in person, it can be seen that the practice was definitely on the decline. Only one incumbent was absent from the united diocese, another was 'about to reside; just appointed'. A great deal of the credit for this improvement must be ascribed to a forgotten milestone in the history of the establishment – the act 13&14 Victoria cap. 98 section 13 by which the holding of more than one benefice with cure of souls was declared illegal.[45]

The whereabouts of incumbents whose absence can be classed as dereliction of duty rather than as a product of organisational eccentricity needs some investigation. In 1806 James Hewetson of Rossmire was living in the diocese of Down on his other benefice. The Hon. and Revd Richard Ponsonby vicar of Mothel and Fews 1800–10 and vicar of Tallow 1817–28 never resided on either and was a noted pluralist.[46] He was preferred to the bishopric of Killaloe in 1828 and was translated to the very rich see of Derry three years later. Primate Alexander, who served as one of his parish priests, described him as 'a prelate of delightful manners and peculiar kindness if not very laborious or pre-eminently spiritually minded'.[47] Standish Grady, vicar of Carrick, was the only absentee in 1806 to arouse the wrath of Bishop Trench who wrote: 'he does not reside, nor do I know where he does reside; but by a letter I have lately received from him, he promises to take up his residence in Carrick in a few days.'[48] One of the worst cases of non-residence was that of Dr Henry Stewart, vicar of Mothel 1810–54 and rector of Loughgilly in the diocese of Armagh 1817–40.[49] Mothel had a church, glebe-house and one of the best incomes in the diocese yet for the first 54 years of the century, its parish priest was always an absentee. Stewart lived at Loughgilly[50] and enjoyed the very large annual income of £1,999 net.[51] Although he felt it necessary to resign Loughgilly in 1840 he retained Mothel until his death in Dublin in 1854 aged 93.[52] Robert Shaw, vicar of Kilsheelan 1829–49, had no church and about 1838 he had no curate,[53] and was living at Carrick (six miles away) but had 22 Protestant parishioners[54] and an annual income of £707 net.

Bishop Bourke in 1819 gave his brother the Hon. George Theobald Bourke the living of Ardfinnan, on which he never resided.[55] He had another living, Kilmacow near Waterford though in the diocese of Ossory, which he looked after in person and where he died in 1847.[56] Together with the precentorship he enjoyed an annual income of £1,031 net out of which he paid his curate at Ardfinnan £75.[57] William French, rector of Lisronagh 1807–63, was non-resident throughout[58] despite the fact that a church was built in 1832 and that in 1836 he had 33 Protestants parishioners.[59] In 1819 he became incumbent of Tibohine in the diocese of Elphin and was 'constantly resident in the glebe-house' having previously been curate at £75 a year.[50] His income from Tibohine was £242 which together with £231 from Lisronagh made a comfortable sum.[61] At this time the prebendary of Donoughmore lived in the glebe-house of that parish about a mile from Lisronagh church and, as the prebendary's church had been a ruin for centuries, French employed him as curate of Lisronagh at £75 a year.[62] The more defensible form of pluralism was represented by the appointment of George Wogan, curate of Donnybrook, Dublin, to the vicarage of the churchless parish of Kilmolash in 1818. His salary as curate was £85 and as his vicarage was 'under the value of £100' he was not a very bloated pluralist.[63]

A summary of non-residence in the diocese of Limerick, Ardfert and Aghadoe also gives a balanced view of the subject as regards Lismore diocese:

> Of many of the clergy who are here returned as not residing on their benefices, it will be seen that many are virtually resident. In all cases of real absence their places are supplied by licensed curates. In several cases where the Incumbent does not reside the value of the parish is very small and insufficient for the support of a clergyman.[64]

Unfortunately, this concern to see that the duties of absentees were properly discharged by deputy developed into a belief that if the duty was provided for, then the absence of the incumbent could not be a subject for adverse comment.[65]

In the 19th century curates were more often employed as substitutes for non-resident incumbents than as assistants in the discharge of heavy parochial duties. In 1807 only two resident incumbents – those of Stradbally and Clonmel – had the assistance of resident curates.[66] Clonmel the parish with the largest population in the diocese seems in fact to always have had a resident incumbent and curate – from at least 1833 it had two curates. In 1807 apart from nominal payments to neighbouring clergymen for discharge of occasional duties, the lowest salary paid to a curate was £50. Six received this sum; one got £65; one £70; four got £75 and one got £90.[67] This compares favourably with the position of curates in England where in 1802 Parson Woodforde paid his curate only £30 a year.[68] Besides, two of the curates in 1807 also possessed vicarages that were, for practical purposes, sinecures. John Lymberg curate to the absent vicar of Rossmire at £65 was also incumbent of the adjoining churchless benefice of Kilbarrymeaden at £85. John Averill was living in Mothel glebe-house as curate to the non-resident vicar at a salary of £70 a year and was also vicar of the churchless parish of Colligan with an income of less than £30 a year.[69] In 1833 there were 21 curates in the diocese[70] 17 of these received £75 p.a.; three, £80; and one £90.[71] Of these two were employed by the vicars choral for Cappoquin and Mocollop and only 8 out of the remaining 19 employers were resident.[72] Some of the curates were obviously permanent and had managed to increase their incomes with sinecures. William Stephenson was curate of Clonmel for 50 years and at the time of his retirement in 1836 he was also prebendary and vicar of Tullaghorton and chaplain to the prison and the garrison at Clonmel.[73] Thomas Parks, curate to the vicars choral 1818–39, was also vicar of Kilmolash from 1831.[74] James Hill was curate for the treasurer at Tullaghmelan from 1812 until 1850 and from 1819 was also vicar of the adjoining churchless parish of Newcastle whose few Protestant parishioners could without much hardship, attend Tullaghmelan church.

Immediately before disestablishment there were only 11 curates in the diocese.[75] The two curates of Clonmel seem to have fared badly – £130 between them while the curate of Tullaghmelan was next with £75 and held no other emoluments. Of the remainder, two were at £100 a year; two at £90 a year; three at £80 and one 'for Sunday duty' at £30 a year. This was Richard Woods, vicar of the neighbouring churchless parish of Lisgenan from which, after expenses including £15 for a house, he had an annual income of £12. He was also a vicar choral of the cathedral.[76] In view of their plentiful supply throughout the 19th century it was probably true that curates were 'as well, or better paid than any gentleman on his entrance into any other profession.'[77]

To summarize the character of the incumbents and curates who served in the diocese between 1801 and 1869 would be an impossible task for one of their most prominent characteristics was their diversity both in personal ability and in the extent to which they discharged their duties. But most of them shared one characteristic. Sykes has said that 'the unreformed Georgian Church did not question the inherited medieval tradition that ecclesiastical revenues existed for the support of ecclesiastical persons irrespective of their residence in the locality from which their revenues were drawn'.[78] The same words could equally well be applied to the incumbents and curates of the diocese of Lismore during the last phase of the establishment.

5. Church buildings

In 1746 there were 16 churches in repair in the diocese.[1] Of these perhaps the most important architecturally was the parish church of Saint Mary, Clonmel. It was a perpendicular building of the late 14th century[2] and it was esteemed 'one of the most magnificent ecclesiastical structures in the country.'[3] In fact, this structure 'half church half fortress'[4] seems to have been more picturesque than beautiful. Of no great height it had square piers and plain arches but it was redeemed by fine windows in the chancel and west front.[5] In 1805 major alterations were made. The choir was shortened by 29 feet and the present porch constructed at the west end, largely from the materials of the White mortuary chapel (1622) while the top storey of the tower was replaced by the present octagonal structure.[6] To provide increased accommodation, this venerable building was, in 1857, re-built out of almost all recognition to the designs of Welland, architect to the Ecclesiastical Commissioners – only the east and west windows, the chancel arch, the base of the tower, the walls of the aisles, and the embattled priest's lodging to the north-east, are incorporated in the present building. A resolution adopted by the committee of parishioners charged with oversight of the work, displays a pathetic belief that Welland's Work could be made to approximate to its 14th-century predecessor:

> With respect to the appearance of the church they see no reason why the present style of the building should not be retained and they suggest that on erecting new Pillars and Arches on the site of the present Pillars and Arches the mouldings and ornaments should be in character with mouldings and ornaments of the arches in the Chancel which would greatly improve the general appearance of the Church and be much more consistent in character without being necessarily of a more expensive description.[7]

Churches wholly built and supported by local magnates were not as common a feature in Ireland as in England. For political reasons, the post-reformation landlord did not live on his country estates among a contented peasantry professing the same religion as himself and for whom he would naturally come to provide a place of worship. In Ireland a change of government meant a corresponding change of landlord who had little opportunity or wish, to develop his estates. By the 18th century when the country houses were going up, the alienation of the popish tenant from his landlord (always given the duplicate title 'English Protestant') was complete. Members of the established church were few, and both they and the landlord were happy to see the Roman Catholic inhabitants of the parish being levied for the erection of their church, notwithstanding the mean and makeshift appearance, which was usually the result of this procedure. Perhaps this lack, in Ireland, of churches, built or furnished in the 18th century may also be due to the absence of village communities around churches[8] or to the destructive tendencies of the 19th century[9] or to lack of piety among the 18th century gentry.[10]

Clonegam parish church and Villierstown chapel are the only places of worship in the diocese whose structures have remained substantially unchanged since the time of their erection in the mid-18th century: the vestry book of Clonegam[11] gives a succinct account of the church's origin.

A Vestry Book
For
The Church of Clonegam
Which was Consecrated
By his Grace the Lord
Arch Bishop of Cashel
June 28th and in year 1741
The Church was built by the
Right Honorable Lord Viscount Tyrone.[12]

It was described by Charles Smith in his account of Waterford soon after its consecration:

> The church of Clonegam ... stands on a hill about a mile to the E. of the house Curraghmore. It is a neat building in good proportion, the floor paved with marble, and within the rails of the altar, with oak in which are handsome veneerings in several geometrical figures. The altar-piece and pulpit are of mahogany and the seats plain and neat. The walls are partly wainscoted and stuc'd, the ceiling neatly garnished with fret-work, and the whole being well lighted, has an elegant appearance. From the door is an extended prospect of the improvements of Curraghmore and a large tract of country on all sides.[13]

There were only 18 Protestant families in the parish c.1766[14] and as the church had accommodation for 200[15] it left plenty of room for improvement – a hope which was fulfilled by 1836 when the parish had 245 Protestant parishioners.[16] In 1825 a cotton-spinning industry was established at Portlaw by the Malcomson family who were Quakers. Their ideas of home-planning were far in advance of their time and streets of model dwellings were laid out for their employees. The new town was situated in no less than three parishes – Clonegam, Guilcagh and Kilmeaden. However, most of it was in Clonegam parish and its church was the one which the townspeople would naturally attend. Since the church was about two miles uphill from Portlaw and the majority of the parishioners were now employed in the factory there, a new church with seating for 300 in the town of Portlaw was consecrated on 6 September 1852.[17] In most similar cases the old church would have been pulled down and its materials either sold or used in the construction of its successor but in this case the old church was retained and has come to be regarded as the private property of the Beresford family by whom it is used as a mortuary chapel.

Villierstown chapel was the foundation of a family that on a famous occasion in the 19th century was successfully to oppose the Beresfords. A chapelry within the benefice of Affane it was founded by John Villiers, 5th earl of Grandison, to minister to a Protestant colony[18] which Lewis in 1837 described as a 'remarkably neat village beautifully situated near the river Blackwater and close to the demesne of Dromana, comprising forty-one houses.'[19] The chapel dates from 1760.[20] It is a spacious cruciform building without tower or spire and it accommodated 400. The interior woodwork was its most noteworthy feature.

Although the history of the established church in the 19th century tends to be one of decline, the building of churches was an activity in which it displayed an unbounded and surprising energy. Church building was greatly encouraged by 42 George III. cap. 108 and by 48 George III. cap. 65. By the latter increased funds were granted to the board of first fruits with which to make grants for building churches and the acts restraining the building of churches in parishes in which there was no public service for the previous 20 years were repealed. 'This system of issuing monies by way of loans repayable by annual instalments at low rate of interest, has tended, more than any other to promote church building in Ireland.'[21] As a result, Ireland was covered with a grid of plain little edifices in 'churchwarden' gothic. It was a last gallant attempt of the Irish church to be the church of all the people and to ensure that nowhere was more than a couple of miles from a church. However, this meant that many country clergymen had fewer than 50 Protestant parishioners.[22] The post-disestablishment church to combat a shortage of priests and falling numbers, has increasingly come to adopt a congregational rather than a territorial system. The result is that the majority of the plain little country churches are at the present time being demolished after little more than a century of usefulness. The diocese of Lismore was no exception to the building movement. The number of churches rose from 16 in 1746 to 36 at disestablishment and of the latter number, none dated to any considerable extent from earlier than *c.*1790.[23] This demonstrates an unfortunate tendency to build new churches rather than to repair existing buildings. All the 16 parish churches in repair in the mid-18th century were either demolished to make way for new buildings or re-built out of all recognition in the 19th. At Ardmore the choir of the cathedral church of Bishop Moelettrim (d. 1203)[24] remained in use until 1838,[25] when, for no good reason, a new church was built and both the oldest church-building and Christian site in the diocese were lost forever to the Irish church. The old church was and remains an interesting building even in ruins. The choir is joined to the Romanesque nave by a 'transitional chancel arch of striking character and considerable beauty'. The external face of the west gable is broken up into a series of arcades and panels, filled with sculptured figures in the style of the high crosses. In the 18th century, at least, the splendid round tower beside the church may have been used as a belfry.[26] In 1829 the arrival of a new vicar coincided with the passing of this resolution at a meeting of the vestry:

> That the present Church is so much out of repair as to be almost unfit for the celebration of Divine Service, that it would be a waste of money to expend any on the repairs of the same – that a New Church shall be erected on another site, the present one being inconvenient.[27]

However, eight years later it was still possible for the vestry to hold their annual meeting in the old church, and the only repairs from which it had benefited during that time was the expenditure of £6. 12s. on the roof and walls in 1830.[28] The vestry had applied originally to the board of first fruits for a loan of £800. Finally the new church was built by the ecclesiastical commissioners and consecrated in 1841.[29] Private funds accounted for £225 of the total cost and this sum would probably have been ample to preserve the old church.

Bishop Stock (1810–13) recognized the foolishness of this passion for new churches in all cases and waged unsuccessful warfare against it. On 22 May 1811 he visited Affane church:

> which we found in some danger of ruin by the bad building of the side wall, though propt on the south by two buttresses. Tenderness for the feelings of the incumbent, old Mr Jessop, in whose time the church was new built about twenty eight years since, was said to prevent an application from the parishioners to have a new church: but the present may stand many years, with a little care and expense.[30]

Stock died in 1813, Prebendary Jessop three years later and in 1820 a new church was consecrated,[31] for whose erection the board of first fruits had given a loan of £500.[32] Thus within the space of 100 years, three churches had been in existence.[33] The bishop visited the town of Cahir on 28 May 1811 and remarked, 'Church at Cahir easily repairable, if the restless desire of some principal parishioners to have the site altered be resisted, as it ought to be.'[34] An unusually large loan of £2,307 was granted by the board of first fruits[35] and a new church was consecrated on 14 February 1820 under the title of 'St John of Cahir'.[36] It is sumptuous little building designed by John Nash[37] in 'Strawberry Hill' gothic and placed in an unrivalled position beside the river Suir. It is said that Nash having completed nearby Shanbally castle for Lord Lismore, Lord Cahir determined to outdo his neighbour by getting Nash to design a much finer building, not for himself but for God. Shanrahan furnishes a later example of refusal to repair an old church, perhaps with some justification in this case. In 1836 it was returned as 'much in want of repair but the vicar refused to expend the grant of sixty pounds last year, in prospect of a new church, the present one being inconvenient to the majority of the parishioners.'[38]

The majority of the present churches were built in the period 1810–35 and most of them to the design of James Pain, junior, architect both to the diocese and to the board of first fruits of Munster.[39] All of these are in an unimaginative simplified gothic relieved by variation more in building material and size than in style. Most of the churches take the shape of a small rectangle, with either four or seven windows, a western tower, never surmounted by a spire and no chancel.[40] St Catherine's, Derrygrath (consecrated 1817) was of special significance, for it retained its fine Regency box pews and an east window displaying a crown, a cross and a chalice, which must have been unusual symbols in a pre-Tractarian Irish country church. Less than half a dozen churches were built in the latter part of our period mainly because sufficient had by then been provided but also because of the system of granting substantial loans for building repayable by the parish over a long period, had been abolished with the board of first fruits.[41] Churches were henceforth built by the ecclesiastical commissioners who required a considerable sum to be raised in local subscriptions before they would commence the work. The churches of Ardmore, Carrick and Shanrahan were re-built by the commissioners, the respective contribution from 'private funds' being £225; £294; and £300. The churches of Dunhill and Rathronan were built exclusively from private funds, the cost of the former being £500 and that of the latter unknown. In one entry it is stated that the drastic enlargement of Clonmel was done exclusively from private funds at a cost of £750, yet another entry states that it was carried out by the commissioners with a local contribution of only £100.[42] Apart from the re-building of St Mary's, Clonmel, by Welland in 1856,[43] the only major constructions were new churches for Shanrahan and Guilcagh. The first, built in the town of Clogheen 1845–6 to the design of James Pain is an uninteresting towerless barn that had seating for 300.[44] The second, Guilcagh, is more interesting. It was designed by William Tinsley who had succeeded Pain as diocesan architect c.1841–4, though he had shared in the erection of Lisronagh and Shanrahan churches as builder.[45] Tinsley's work was in many respects unique in the diocese. The most noticeable novelty was the tiled roof, another was the use of a bell turret instead of the usual tower. The foundation stone was laid in 1849 by George Wilson, a parishioner who, if the stone is to be believed, was then 106 years of age, and the church was erected by Louisa wife of the third marquess of Waterford. Lady Waterford is believed to have defrayed the cost out of her pocket money. Although the church was only about two miles from Portlaw, there were 60 Protestant parishioners in 1861. Lady Waterford also had a share in the provision of the new church at Portlaw in her own parish of Clonegam. Bishop Daly, probably from 'low church' prejudices, forbade 'picture windows' but the marchioness designed the east window 'of pleasing colour in strict compliance with the bishop's wishes'. The other windows were decorated with narrow ribands displaying biblical texts.[46]

The furnishing of churches 'with things necessary for the celebration of Divine Service, preaching, and administration of the Sacraments' was governed by canon law.[47] If church building was a distinguishing characteristic of the 19th-century church, the provision of good altar plate was a notable achievement in many places during the 18th and to a lesser extent, the 17th century. In the diocese of Lismore there are five sets of chalice and paten dating from the 17th century[48] and nine sets from the 18th.[49]

At the end of the 18th century, the conditions of the church interior and its fittings could vary widely. Rossmire had no plate or linen in 1793 or 1796.[50] Ardfinnan was in 'general good repair' in 1790 except that the surplice had been stolen out of the church 'but a new one preparing',[51] but only six years later the pews, pulpit and communion table were described as 'rotten'.[52] Disert was almost as bad as possible, 'not sashed or floored, no pulpit or pews'.[53] Criticisms were not quite as startling as this in 1836. Only six churches were in bad structural repair.[54] New books were needed in seven churches;[55] the surplice was either bad or altogether lacking in five cases.[56] Templemichael and the porch of Monksland needed to be white-washed. A bell was required in Templemichael and Tubrid and a font in Shanrahan. Rossmire had only managed to obtain a pewter chalice and two patens, 'not fit for use' while Ringagoonagh had no plate whatever.[57]

An indignant resolution adopted by the vestry of Inishlounaght parish on 1 February 1819 shows that the hazards to which churches are subject, have changed little:

> We the Clergyman, Churchwardens and parishioners being duly assembled and seeing with just abhorrence the Outrage that has been committed by some person or persons unknown in breaking the windows of the church and schoolhouse have Resolved that the sum of ten pounds be applotted on the Parish for the purpose of repairing the same and offering a Reward for the discovery and prosecution of so sacrilegious and Scandalous and Outrage.[58]

It is clear that at least during the first half of the century the altar was covered with a 'carpet' as required by the canon and never left bare in the modern manner. Nor had hideous brass book-stands replaced the cushion on altar and pulpit. In 1790 it was reported that Cahir had 'no covering for the communion table but a linen one ... no cushion for that or the pulpit'. Ardfinnan had both a red cloth and 'linen' (for use at Holy Communion). In 1796 a cover for the communion table was bought for Clonmel. In 1790 the interior of Rathronan was reported thus; 'a good reading desk without any cover, pulpit good, communion table old and bad without carpet or any other covering except good linen ... No cushions around rail of communion table'. The churchwardens of Clashmore were ordered in 1820 to provide a pulpit-cushion for the new church. In 1829 a green cloth was obtained for the communion table in Ardmore at a cost of 6s. In 1824 the churchwardens of Clonmel were ordered 'to provide a carpet for the Communion Table and to cover the Chancel Door with Green Cloth and a deeper curtain to the East Window'[59] 'Cushions and trimmings for the pulpit and reading desk and a cloth for the communion table' were 'much wanted' at Kilrossanty in 1836.[60]

The seating of churches underwent a revolution during the later 19th century, the square box pews making way for the form of seating now customary.[61] Pews were regarded as the private property of their occupiers. A major item of business at vestry meetings was registering the sales of pews that had occurred during the previous year. An entry in Clonmel vestry book for 1817 is paralleled by many similar entries in the other vestry books: 'Ordered that the pew in the north gallery next the organ, heretofore the property of the parish be now the property of William Riall Esq., he having purchased the same from the parish for the sum of fifteen guineas.'[62] Pew owners were also responsible for the repairs to their own pews. In 1815 Carrick vestry transferred a pew to a new owner 'previous owner not resident herein for several years and it having been repaired by the parish'. In Clonmel in 1820 pew number 33 was given as 'bishop's throne'. In Dungarvan at the beginning of the century a pew on the south side was similarly designated.[63] The result of this trade in pews was that many families had no opportunity of securing one even if they had the means to do so. There was always a certain number of 'parish' pews but they tended to diminish by sale and they also bore the significant alternative title of 'poor pews.' In Clonmel parish in 1855 64 church families had no pews in the parish church and depended on accommodation 'in some cases willingly given by their friends – in others on chance seats provided by the sexton' and 21 families of that number absented themselves altogether on the plea of not having seats. Even the clergy of the parish had to buy pews for their families.[64] The need for increased accommodation was often the factor responsible for the sweeping away of the square pews[65] but they also had the disadvantage that 'the congregation in a great proportion of the sittings have their backs to the officiating minister and many in the gallery and Back Aisles situated behind the pillars cannot see the Reading Desk at all – and some hear but imperfectly.'[66] A courageous decision was made about the seating in the church of Carrick, re-built in 1839,[67] by which the families were no longer to have power to dispose of their seats and a meeting of the congregation was held to distribute sittings 'according to the discretion of the bishop'.[68] In the years immediately preceding disestablishment, a period during which many people would hold taste in church architecture and furniture to be at its lowest ebb, a movement arose in the diocese to re-model the interiors of the churches and its pace was quickened when the restraints of the establishment were removed. An admirer of this trend stated, 'the difficulty would be to mention one church which did not benefit from the voluntary and spontaneous desire of the members of the church in the diocese to beautify and adorn the temples of God'. The following churches 'were provided with additional accommodation by the alteration of pews and fittings' 1860–7: Stradbally, Tubrid and Tullaghmelan. The work was carried out by the ecclesiastical commissioners and the respective amounts contributed in private subscriptions were £50; £7; and £78. A resolution of Ardmore vestry in 1883 is an indication of the disrepute into which the fittings of even 40 years before had fallen: 'The question of re-modelling the church pews to some proper shape and height, as pew seats are now made, was brought before the meeting. It was generally conceded that such would be a very great improvement'. It was decided that efforts should be made to get new sittings and that these efforts were successful is only too obvious today. A specimen of the former seating remains in the gallery and in the two tiny transepts.[69] Only one church (Cahir) today retains distinctively early 19th-century fittings.

The erection of glebe-houses, as of churches, is largely an achievement of the early 19th century. An Act of 1808[70] provided better facilities for grants and loans than those acts hitherto in force.[71] These inducements to build were widely availed of until they were withdrawn under the Church Temporalities Act.[72] In 1768 there were only three glebe-houses in the diocese.[73] By 1837 there were 15 houses[74] and of these 11 had been built under the new Act of 1808. In 1867 the number of houses had risen to 22,[75] yet there were 36 churches and 41 benefices. The fact that these three figures were not identical was, to a certain extent, a measure of the failure of the church establishment.

Notes

ABBREVIATIONS

Cotton, *Fasti*	Henry Cotton, *Fasti ecclesiae Hibernicae* (6 vols, Dublin, 1851–78)
DNB	*Dictionary of National Biography*
Est. ch.	*Report of H.M. commissioners on the revenue and condition of the established church (Ireland)* HC 1867–8 (4082) xxiv
H.C.	Parliamentary papers, house of Commons series
2nd rep	*Second report of his majesty's commissioners on ecclesiastical revenue and patronage in Ireland*, HC 1834 (589), xxiii
3rd rep	*Third report of his majesty's commissioners on ecclesiastical revenue and patronage in Ireland*, HC 1836 (246), xxv
4th rep	*Fourth report of his majesty's commissioners on ecclesiastical revenue and patronage in Ireland*, HC 1837 (500), xxv
RCB	Representative Church Body Library, Dublin
TCD	Trinity College, Dublin

INTRODUCTION

1 P. Power, *Waterford and Lismore* (Dublin and Cork, 1937), p. 1; W.H. Rennison, *Succession list of the bishops, cathedral and parochial clergy of the diocese of Waterford and Lismore* (Waterford, 1920), p. 7.
2 Ibid.
3 Rennison, *Succession list*, pp 7–8.
4 Power, *Waterford and Lismore*, p. 4.
5 Rennison, *Succession list*, p. 34.
6 D.A. Beaufort, *Memoir of a map of Ireland* (London, 1792), p. 103.
7 *Abstract of the returns made in pursuance of the acts for taking a census of the population of Ireland 1831*, p. 190 (634) HC 1833, xxxix, p. 252.
8 RCB, Rural dean's report, 1836. Today there are less than 100.
9 S. Lewis, *Topographical dictionary of Ireland* (2 vols, London, 1837), i. p. 369.
10 *Abstract of ... census of the population of Ireland, 1831*, p. 252.
11 RCB, Rural dean's report, 1836.
12 E. Wakefield, *An account of Ireland, statistical and political* (3 vols, London, 1812), i. p. 75.
13 *Abstract of ... census of the population of Ireland, 1831*, p. 252.
14 RCB, Rural dean's report, 1836. Today there are none.

15 *Abstract of ... census of the population of Ireland 1831*, p. 266.
16 RCB, Rural dean's report, 1836.
17 Wakefield, *Account*, i, pp 77, 278.
18 Beaufort, *Memoir*, p. 101.
19 R.B. McDowell, *Public opinion and government policy in Ireland, 1801–1846* (London, 1952), p. 19.
20 'Register of baptisms, parish of Tallow' in the possession of the dean of Lismore; Vestry book 1813–1916' formerly in the possession of the rector of Killaloan; Register 1827–45 of the parish of Clonegam.
21 D.A. Doudney, *A pictorial outline of the rise and progress of the Bonmahon industrial, infant and agricultural schools, county of Waterford* (Bonmahon, 1855), p. 8.
22 H. Madden, *Memoir of the Rt Revd Robert Daly* (London, 1875), p. 275. Bishop Daly's comment was 'I wish they could see their ugly child.'
23 Doudney, *Pictorial outline*, p. 24.
24 Ibid.
25 Ibid.
26 Ibid., p. 28. The last service in Monksland church was held on 6 June 1937 in the presence of seven people (Preacher's book of the parish of Stradbally).

27 McDowell, *Public opinion*, pp 33–4.
28 J.T. Ball, *The reformed church of Ireland,
    1537–1886* (London and Dublin, 1886),
    p. 243.
29 *Papers accompanying the report of H.M.
    Commissioners for inquiry into endowed
    schools in Ireland*, pp 362–413 (2336) HC
    1857–8, xxxii (part iv), pp 366–417.
30 T. Olden, *The church of Ireland* (London,
    1892), p. 395.
31 Letter 4 April 1832 among MSS of the
    dean of Lismore. The corps of the
    deanery of Lismore was the rectory of
    Tubrid in Co. Tipperary.
32 Power, *Waterford and Lismore*, p. 67.

1. THE BISHOPS

1 Augustus Theiner (ed.), *Vetera monumenta
   Hibernorum et Scotorum, 1216–1547*
   (Rome, 1864), p. 311
2 Rennison, *Succession list*, p. 25.
3 Cotton, *Fasti*, i, p. 124).
4 TCD, MS 947, 21 Mar. 1810.
5 *First report of the commissioners on
   ecclesiastical revenue and patronage in Ireland*
   (762), HC 1833, xxi, p. 243.
6 *Est. ch.*, p. 9
7 Michael Mac Donagh (ed.) *The viceroy's
   post-bag* (London, 1904), p. 121.
8 The other was Dickson of Down and
   Connor (W. Alison Phillips (ed.), *History
   of the Church of Ireland* (3 vols, Oxford,
   1933), iii, p. 271).
9 Henry Grattan, *Memoirs of the life and
   times of the Rt. Hon. Henry Grattan*
   (5 vols, London, 1839–46), i, p. 41.
10 Cotton, *Fasti* iiii, 173.
11 At his triennial visitation of the diocese
    in 1802 Archbishop Broderick, on a
    review of the reports before him,
    declared 'that he observed little to
    commend' (J.D. Sirr, *Memoir of the
    Honorable and Most Reverence Power le Poer
    Trench, last archbishop of Tuam* (Dublin,
    1845) p. 28).
12 Francis Hardy, *Memoirs of the political and
    private life of James Caulfield earl of
    Charlemont* (London, 1810), p. 14.
13 Sirr, *Memoir*, p. 25.
14 TCD, MS 947, 23 May 1810.
15 His father, grandfather and brother had
    all been MP for Co. Galway. His father
    was given a barony in 1797, a viscountcy
    in 1801, and the earldom of Clancarty in
    1803 – a significant time for such rapid

promotions. His mother was the
daughter of Luke Gardiner, Viscount
Mountjoy (Burke).
16 At Trinity College, Dublin (Sirr, *Memoir*,
    p. 5).
17 This was the union of Creagh in the
    diocese of Clonfert that contained the
    great fair-town of Ballinasloe (ibid., p. 9).
    In 1793 he was given the living of
    Rawdenstown in the diocese of Meath,
    but continued to hold Creagh by faculty.
18 Ibid., p. 10.
19 Ibid., p. 12. He was agent to his father
    and was also a justice of the peace, and
    captain of the yeomanry. After his
    marriage in 1795 he became agent to his
    father-in-law at Castle Taylor about 15
    miles from Ballinasloe (ibid. p. 13).
20 Ibid., pp 19–20.
21 Mac Donagh, *The viceroy's post-bag*,
    pp 43, 96, 120–1.
22 Sirr, *Memoir*, p. 25.
23 Ibid.
24 'It cannot be fairly asserted … that he
    entered on the high office of bishop
    with strictly spiritual views; but he
    undertook it in the steadfast purpose of
    discharging its duties vigilantly and
    effeciently' (ibid., p. 27).
25 Ibid., p. 26
26 In particular, Kilrossanty (ibid., p. 24) and
    Cappoquin (TCD, MS 948).
27 Sirr, *Memoir*, p. 29.
28 *Papers relating to the established church in
    Ireland*, pp 222–33 HC 1807, v.
29 After making many sensible and
    imaginative suggestions about the
    arrangement of benefices and the siting
    of new churches, he adds a very humble
    postscript: 'Though I have taken great
    pains in making the foregoing arrange-
    ments of the parishes within this diocese;
    yet it is possible that upon revising, it,
    may admit of much alteration.'
30 His successor Joseph Stock bishop of
    Killala has left a frank account of how
    the translation was effected: 'I had your
    notice of the defection of Lord Ely (his
    son was bishop of Killaloe) on account
    of the preference given to the bishop of
    Waterford by the Lord Lieutenant but
    you did not … tell me … that the duke
    (of Richmond) had actually let slip in
    conversation his having actually
    promised Elphin to the Frenchs …
    (TCD, MS 947, 9 Feb. 1810).

31 *DNB*. Dr Stock, perhaps inevitably in a successor, was on bad terms with him and described him as a 'narrow-minded man' (TCD, MS 947, 26 May 1811).

32 Ibid.

33 Alison Phillips (ed.) *History of the Church of Ireland*, iii, p. 343.

34 TCD, MS 947.

35 'A distinguished Hebraist and noted for his translation of the book of Job into English' R. Mant, *History of the Church of Ireland* (2 vols, London, 1840), ii, p. 742.

36 'Among the remainder occur the respectable names of O'Beirne, Stock and Young of whom it is to be presumed, that their elevation was due to their personal merit. Bishop Stock, it may be incidentally noticed, was a brother-in-law of Primate Newcome' (Mant, *History*, ii, p. 771).

37 *A narrative of what passed at Killala in the summer of 1798, By an eye-witness* (Dublin 1800).

38 Fox tried unsuccessfully to have him promoted in 1806 (Henry Richard Fox 3rd baron Holland) *Memoirs of the whig party during my time* (London, 1852), i, p. 136) see also: J.T. Gilbert, *A history of the city of Dublin* (3 vols, Dublin, 1859), ii, p. 308 and R.B. McDowell (ed.), *Social life in Ireland, 1800–45* (Dublin, 1957), p. 34.

39 TCD, MS 947.

40 TCD, MS 947, 14 Mar. 1813.

41 Gilbert, *History of the city of Dublin*, ii, p. 308.

42 TCD, MS 947, 16 May 1810. He lamented 'I shall be left with a house not one quarter furnished. For a table in the study covered with black leather, I have been obliged to pay fourteen pounds and for two arm chairs ... ten pounds each'.

43 TCD, MS 947, 23 May 1810.

44 TCD, MS 947, 19 Oct 1810: 'My gout is gone and my rents, I hope, are coming in. so in pretty good spirits'. In the following month he set off to visit parts of Lismore diocese which he had not yet seen (TCD, MS 947, 9 Nov.) – a not – inconsiderable undertaking for an old man in winter. He was troubled with gout all through the spring of 1811 but on May 8 he writes: 'I am quite well of the gout and waiting for weather to begin my progress through the diocese of Lismore.'

45 For example his comment on Whitechurch: 'Found it very decent and in good condition, only the west side rendered damp by a vestibule invented by the incumbent with no great show of genius'. (TCD, MS 948, 22 May 1811).

46 TCD, MS 947, 15 May 1811. He appointed his eldest son, Edwin, prebendary of Errew and vicar of Crossmolina in Killala diocese, at the age of 22 in 1831. He preferred his son-in-law Henry Palmer to the benefice of Tubrid in Lismore diocese which he was to hold for 54 years. It was one of the better living; in 1831 its net income was £550 (*4th rep*). He also put forward an unsuccessful scheme for endowing his invalid son Charles with part of the salary of the Diocesan Registrar (TCD, MS 947, 15 May).

47 TCD, MS 947, 11 Nov 1811. 'But God knows what I can do, harassed as I am here with providing for four sons at once, who, by the way seem well enough inclined to believe my resources are inexhaustible'.

48 TCD, MS 947, 16 May 1810.

49 Boulston Lodge, Haverfordwest. (TCD, MS 947, 8 Aug. 1810).

50 TCD, MS 947, 17 Oct. 1810.

51 'Creep on by degrees to the comforts of life and you will have the best chance of not repenting of their cost' (TCD, MS 947, 5 May 1813) and; 'Go on, lads, and prosper in mutual peace and harmony, prays your father, who has himself through life experienced the advantage of sacrificing very much to the preservation of peace with all his connections' (TCD, MS 947, 14 Jun 1813).

52 TCD, MS 948, 20 May 1811 and 29 May 1811.

53 'Enquire after Shiell's widow ... and let me know how I may relieve her, if she appears to deserve relief. Poor Shiell taught you all very well to write and was a harmless insufficient creature' (TCD, MS 947, 10 Apr. 1813).

54 'Harry, I would not forbear to enquire after the Orphans of that poor woman Mrs Shiell, now that nobody is left to look after them. Their condition must be most destitute. Act for me as if I were on the spot and I shall thank you. A penny well bestowed in this life will be well

worth a shilling in the next says the
considerate lover of money. We are busy
this day carrying to the cellar a Pipe of
Port from Grubb the Quaker Wine
Merchant at Clonmel, a man whose
candid dealings I like' (TCD, MS 947, 18
June 1813).

55 TCD, MS 947, 22 Dec. 1812.
56 TCD, MS 947, 8 Jul. 1813.
57 1791. Prebendary of Killabegs in Tuam
cathedral, rector of Crossboyne and
Mayo and rector of Athenry (Cotton,
Fasti, iiii, p. 35); 1795 rector of
Templemichael and Mohill; 1800 dean of
Ardagh. From 1798 he was also precentor
of St Patrick's, Dublin (ibid., iii.189).
58 His wife was the daughter of Robert
Fowler, archbishop of Dublin
1779–1801.
59 *Papers relating to the established church in
Ireland*, pp 244–53.
60 J.D. Forbes, *Victorian architect, the life and
work of William Tinsley* (Bloomington,
1953), pp 21–2. The bishop's son and
heir, Robert 5th earl of Mayo was 'a
strong evangelical', ibid., p. 21).
61 3 & 4 William IV., cap. 37.
62 Cotton, *Fasti*, i, p. 24.
63 He read widely in theology and canon
law and in later life he studied oriental
languages. He was also interested in
chemistry.
64 Cotton, *Fasti*, i, p. 28
65 *DNB*
66 Cf. R. Lawrence, A *charge delivered at the
primary triennial visitation of the province of
Munster in the year 1823* (Dublin 1823). In
this he puts forward a vigorous defence
of the existing tithe system and goes into
details of non-residence in his dioceses
in order to refute allegations made in
parliament.
67 J.D. White, *Sixty years in Cashel* (Cashel,
1893), p. 40. Yet the same authority states
that when Dr Stephen Sandes succeeded
Laurence in 1839, he found two priests
in the dioceses of Cashel who had both
been curates for 18 years, one at £150 a
year and the other at £75. Bishop Sandes
forthwith preferred them to benefices
each worth £1000 a year – which might
be regarded as too far, in the opposite
direction but well illustrates the
capricious manner in which patronage
was dispensed under the establishment
(ibid., p. 40).

68 Sirr, *Memoir*, pp 618–19.
69 Order book quoted in RCB, W.M.
Rennison, MS 'History of the dioceses
of Waterford and Lismore 1746–1872'.
This states that 40 children were
confirmed at Ardmore; 70 at Dungarvan;
and 120 at Lismore.
70 *Annual Register 1842*, p. 302.
71 *DNB*
72 His father was the Rt. Hon. Denis Daly
MP of Dunsandle, Go. Galway and his
mother, the only daughter and heiress of
Robert earl of Farnham. The bishop's
brother was in 1845 created Baron
Dunsandle and Clanconal (G.E.
C[ockayne], *The complete peerage* (13 vols,
London, 1910–40), iii, p. 550).
73 In 1803 he graduated from Dublin
University with a gold medal, *Dublin
University calendar* (Dublin 1907), p. 114.
74 He himself subsequently disapproved of
his motives in taking this step for which
he made the arrangements during a ball,
H. Madden, *Memoir of the Right Rev.
Robert Daly D.D. Lord Bishop of Cashel*
(London, 1875), p. 12.
75 Ibid., p. 34.
76 Ibid., p. 65.
77 Ibid., p. 195.
78 Ibid., p. 191. This was a system of
dispatching itinerant missionaries on
organized circuits throughout Ireland
with the prosletyzing of Roman
Catholics as a particular object.
79 Ibid., p. 202.
80 H.J. Lawlor, *Fasti of St Patrick*
(Dublin, 1930), p. 51.
81 Madden, *Memoir*, p. 222.
82 Ibid., pp 224–5.
83 R.S. Brooke, *Recollections of the Irish
Church* (London, 1877), p. 20.
84 Madden, *Memoir*, p. 304.
85 Rennison, *Succession list*, p. 160; Madden,
Memoir, p. 306.
86 White, *Sixty years in Cashel*, p. 38.
87 He had a farm three miles from
Waterford for the purpose of giving
employment (Madden, *Memoir*, p. 60)
88 Ibid., p. 304.
89 James Godkin, *Ireland and her churches*
(London, 1867), p. 224; White, *Sixty years
in Cashel*, p. 40).
90 Godkin, *Ireland and her churches*, p. 324.
91 Brooke, *Recollections*, p. 20.

2. THE CATHEDRAL CHURCH OF ST CARTHAGH

1 Rennison, *Succession list*, pp 180–1 also J. Godfrey F. Day and Henry E. Patton, *The Cathedrals of the church of Ireland* (London and Dublin, 1932), p. 130. Power, *Waterford and Lismore*, p. 220.

2 The circular arch in the nave and some carved stones set into the west wall are twelfth-century and the transept arches to the north and south are of 13th-century work. There is also a very fine 16th-century altar-tomb of the Magrath family 'carved with almost every known symbol of ecclesiastical art' (Day & Patton, *Cathedrals.*, p. 132).

3 'The graceful spire of Lismore church, the prettiest I have seen in, or, I think, out of Ireland' M.A. Titmarsh [W.M. Thackeray], *The Irish sketch-book* (London, 1843), i, p. 93.

4 Charles Smith, *The antient and present state of the county and city of Waterford* (Dublin, 1746), p. 53; Lismore Chapter book 1663–1829, among MSS of the dean of Lismore.

5 Smith, *Antient and present state.* Lismore castle passed into the possession of the Cavendish family on the marriage of the 4th duke of Devonshire in 1748 to Baroness Clifford only surviving daughter and heir of Richard Boyle, earl of Burlington and Cork (C[ockayne], *The complete peerage*, iii, p. 346).

6 Lismore Chapter book, 22 Apr 1807.

7 Lismore Chapter book 10 Sept. 1811; Chapter book 22 July 1814.

8 TCD, MS 948, 21 May 1811; R.H. Hyland, *History, topography, and antiquities of the county and city of Waterford*, (London, 1824) pp 336–7

9 Letter to R.J. Orpen, 17 Sept. 1837 among MSS of the dean of Lismore.

10 Plans for the repair and re-construction of Lismore cathedral drawn up by E.H. Carson, architect (1868) among MSS of the dean of Lismore. 'In making a whole cathedral one unit for worship ... the nineteenth-century was attempting an impossible task ... the congregation can be little more than spectators of the worship offered in the choir', G.W.O. Addleshaw & Frederick Etchells, *The architectural setting of Anglican worship* (London 1948), p. 215. The truth of this contention is demonstrated at Lismore

by the fact that after disestablishment it was found necessary to cut off part of the east end of the building with an oak screen. Yet it was still impossible from the back of the nave to hear what is said at the altar now in front of this screen.

11 Ibid., p. 216.

12 *2nd rep*, 184 and Rennison *Succession list*, p. 51.

13 Sirr, *Memoir*, p. 30; Lismore Chapter book.

14 The dean, precentor (or chanter), chancellor, treasurer, archdeacon and the prebendaries of Tullaghorton, Mora, Disert and Kilmoleran, Donoughmore and Kiltegan, Kilgobinet, Kilrossanty, Modeligo, Seskinan and Clashmore (Chapter book 1663–1829, Cotton *Fasti*, i, pp 164–205). About the middle of the 15th century the rectory of Kilbarrymeaden was erected into a prebend which was assigned to the precentor of Waterford but after 1740 mention of this prebend disappears from the chapter records. The deanery was in the patronage of the crown, the rest in that of the bishop.

15 There were only five larger chapters; St Patrick's Dublin with 26 members; Cloyne with 19; Cork with 17; Limerick with 16; and Ferns with 15, *2nd rep*, p. 113.

16 See Rennison, *Succession list*, pp 51–72.

17 The large-scale restoration 1807–14 and the erection of the tower and spire, 1827, were financed out of the œconomy fund. About 1832 the fund yielded £824 a year (*2nd rep*, p. 95).
 In 1837 the fund was held to be 'not big enough for repairs of the cathedral and to keep up some semblance of a Choir' (letter, Dean Cotton to R.J. Orpen, among MSS of the dean of Lismore).

18 *Papers relating to the established church in Ireland*, p. 222; RCB, Rural dean's report, 1836.

19 This term is used in *Papers relating to the established church in Ireland*, HC 1807, v. The income of the chancellor about 1831 was £129 per annum; that of the prebendary of Modeligo was £180; that of the prebendary of Seskinan was £185; and that of the prebendar of Clashmore was £150. The remaining dignities ranged from £436 to £1,164 p.a. and the remaining prebends from £200 to £400 p.a. (*2nd rep*, p. 97).

20 Letter Dean Dawson to Dean Bishopp 4 April 1831 among MSS of the dean of Lismore.

21 *2nd rep*, p. 185 and *4th rep*, p. 814.

22 *2nd rep*, p., 198 and *4th rep*, pp 730, 548. The prebendary of District and Kilmoleran, Nicholas Herbert, was resident on his benefice of Knockgraffon in Cashel diocese enjoying a net combined income of £1118 per annum (*2nd rep*, p. 262 and *4th rep.*, p. 682).

23 His net income was £231 a year (*4th rep*, p. 736). In 1806 the rectory and vicarage had been permanently untied by act of Council (Rennison, *Succession list* p. 158).

24 *4th rep*, p. 452. From the two preferments he had a joint income of £272 a year.

25 The Hon. John Beresford was son of Archbishop Beresford of Tuam. He was made a deacon at Cloyne in 1803; was rector of Ballynoe and Ahern in that diocese 1806–55 and prebendary of Kilrossanty, 1812–55, none of the appointments carrying cure of souls. He resided in England and had a net annual income of £1121 a year (*4th rep*, pp 745, 92). He succeeded his father as 2nd Lord Decies in 1819 (motto: *nil nisi cruce*). Significantly, his mother was sister of John Fitzgibbon, earl of Clare (C[ockayne], *The complete peerage*, iii, 112).

26 *2nd rep*, p. 184.

27 *2nd rep*, pp 262–4.

28 The deanery was suspended in 1834 but the suspension was removed in 1849; the precentorship became an unendowed dignity in 1849 when the rectorial tithes of Ardmore were annexed to the vicarage. The chancellorship was suspended in 1861; the prebend of Tullghorton in 1836; Mora in 1867; Donoughmore in 1861; Kilgobnet in 1863; Modeligo in 1844; Seskinan in 1851; (Cotton, *Fasti*, i, pp 172–205 and Rennison, *Succession list*, pp 54–73).

29 Ibid. The treasureship, the archdeaconry and the prebends of Disert and Kilmoleran and Clashmore only escaped suspension because they had not become vacant since the passing of the Act.

30 The dean, the Hon. Henry Montague Browne, was resident on his benefice of Burnchurch in the diocese of Ossory the net annual income of which was £520, *Est. ch.*, pp 414–15.

William Mackey was appointed prebendary and vicar of Clashmore in 1827 (Rennison, *Succession list*, pp 73, 127). In 1846 he left the diocese to become incumbent of Drakestown in the diocese of Meath (Irish church directory) but most unsuitably retained the prebend until about 1863 (Rennison, *Succession list*, p. 73).

31 *DNB* sub Henry Cotton; *Catalogue of the books in the diocesan library of Lismore 1851* (Privately published, 1851).

32 *4th rep* p. 744. By a stretch of the imagination it was regarded as the glebe-house of the archdeacon's parish of Kilrush.

33 The monument of archdeacon Ryan (1810–28) in Lismore cathedral records 'he constantly resided in the Archdeaconry House.'

34 William Jessop and vicar choral from 1768 and a prebendary from 1774 (Cotton, *Fasti*, i, p. 209) although beneficed in the diocese from 1769 seems to have spent most of his life at Lismore where he was headmaster of the 'Diocesan School' famous for number of scholars in Mr Jessop's time' (TCD, MS 948, 21 May 1811). In 1807 Bishop Trench reported him as 'being, as is supposed, above eighty years of age, and not having left his house for two years' (*Papers relating to the established church in Ireland*, p. 244). Yet he lived until 1816. In 1811 Bishop Stock visited him at his house in Lismore and in that year and again in 1814 meetings of the chapter were adjourned to it (chapter book). He acted as œconomist for many years and in 1775 was responsible for the introduction of an organ (ibid.). Henry Meyrick vicar choral 1847–87 was prebendary of Modeligo and curate at Lismore for the other vicars 1853–61 (Rennison, *Succession list*, pp 70, 182).

35 Cotton, *Fasti*, i, p. 79. At first the five vicars were presented by the respective dignitaries but from at least the 17th century their appointment was in the hands of the dean (Rennison, *Succession list*, pp 76–7).

36 *2nd rep*, p. 156; Letter, Dean Cotton to R.S. Orpen among MSS of the dean of Lismore; Vicars account book, among MSS of the dean of Lismore.

37　*Papers relating to the established. church in Ireland*, p. 222.. This must have been Thomas Crawford, vicar 1794–1822 and 'curate of Lismore' for 30 years (Cotton, *Fasti*, i, p. 81). He was also headmaster of the diocesan school for in 1811 Bishop Stock remarked that it had 'declined greatly under Mr Crawford, old and deaf' (TCD, MS 948, 21 May 1811).

38　Verney Lovett, D.D. a native of Tipperary and graduate of Trinity College, Cambridge, was a vicar-choral for 44 years 1781–1825 (Cotton, *Fasti* i, p. 210). He was also treasurer of Cork 1795–1815 prebendary of Kilbrogan 1815–18 and rector of Kilnegross 1818–25 (W.M. Brady, *Clerical and parochial records of Cork, Cloyne and Ross* (3 vols, Dublin, 1863), i, pp 23, 143). In 1819 under this head he was returned as 'resident at Lismore'. In 1797 both Crawford and Lovett were present, at a vestry meeting though only the former is designated 'minister'. Philip Ryan vicar 1802–28, was present with Crawford and Lovett at a vestry in 1805 (vestry book 1797–1873 among MSS of the Dean of Lismore). Ryan became also archdeacon in 1810 and certainly from that time resided in the archdeaconry house (monument in the cathedral). Daniel Sullivan, vicar 1807–39 was also for many years preacher to the dean and chapter (i.e. he preached the turns of absent canons). In 1806 before he became vicar, he was elected one of the churchwardens for that year while in 1807 the vestry adjourned to his house (vestry book). He was vicar of Rathronan 1806–20 and of Kilronan 1820–39 and was non-resident in both (*Papers relating to the established church in Ireland*, p. 228, HC 1807, v, and *4th rep*, p. 744).

　　In 1808 the Revd Thomas Parks (curate to the vicars from 1818) was appointed a churchwarden while Dean Scott was sometimes also present at vestries (vestry book). So it would appear as if there were an ample number of clergymen at least living near the cathedral.

39　RCB, Rural dean's report, 1836.

40　*2nd rep*, pp 262–4.

41　He was buried there in 1839 (Cotton, *Fasti*, i, p. 210).

42　Letter, Dean Cotton to R.J. Orpen 17 September 1837 among MSS of the dean of Lismore.

43　Ibid. It should be remembered that Mocollop and Cappoquin were still within the huge parish of Lismore and Mocollop throughout which the vicars-choral had cure of souls.

44　Ibid.

45　Counsel's brief among MSS of the dean of Lismore. The legal costs were £74 4*d.* 6*s.*

46　At every service there were always two vicars present: one to read and the other to preach ('Preacher's book 1843–50' among MSS in the possession of the dean of Lismore).

47　At the instigation of the bishop Revd W.E. Shaw unsuccessfully took legal proceedings in 1850, to establish that Woods had forfeited his place by accepting a benefice with cure of souls (*Ye five clerkes of Lysmore*; copy of chancery petition, Shaw v the Vicars-choral among MSS of the dean of Lismore).

48　*Irish Church directory.*

49　*Est. ch.*, pp 108–9. The annual income of the corporation was £564, thus if the vicars had 'all come back within theyr paryishe boundes' and discharged the duty in person, each would have received £116 not 'full fyftye poundes'. But after paying for the spiritual duties of Lismore and Mocollop, each only received £62 (ibid.). After the death of Power in 1868, no vicar remained at Lismore. Hans Butler, chaplain of Villierstown died in 1891 aged 82; Richard Woods resided near Youghal as being near his churchless parish, Lisgenan and also near Clashmore and Kinsalebeg where he was successively curate. He died in 1886. Samuel Meyrick, incumbent of Blessington and prebendary of Tipperkevin in St Patrick's Dublin died in 1887. Henry Browne son of Dean Browne was vicar of Dungarvan 1854–73. He then became rector of Bredon, Worcestershire and died in 1911.

　　John Bain who succeeded Power as vicar-choral in 1869 was first curate then vicar of Dungarvan and died in 1900 (Rennison, *Succession list*, p. 79 and *Irish church directory*). No vicars have been appointed since the disestablishment.

50 H.A. Boyd, 'The cathedral system in the Church of Ireland since the disestablishment', unpublished B.Litt. thesis, TCD, 1950, p. 323.

51 RCB, Rural dean's report, 1836. Shanrahan was the only other church in the diocese with a week-day service.

52 William Jessop, Vicar-choral 1768–1816 (Chapter book). He also gave £110 towards the purchase of the organ (Cotton, *Fasti*, i, p. 204).

53 Lismore Chapter book.

54 *2nd rep*, pp 262–4. The names of the boys were: Honoria Beville; Ably Huddy; Melsina Beville; Robert Anderson; George Gardiner; William Gardiner; John Clancy.

55 Boyd. 'Cathedral system', p. 41.

3. THE PARISHES, THEIR BOUNDARIES AND INCOMES

1 Power, *Waterford and Lismore*, pp 42–3. Some writers refuse to regard these parishes as, in any sense, ecclesiastical denominations and designate them 'civil parishes' since they continued to be used for purposes of local government until modern times.

2 Rennison, *Succession list*, p. 13. In the Roman catholic Church the old tithes or parishes have been abandoned though in the penal times of the 18th century a determined effort was made to retain them (Power, *Waterford and Lismore*, p. 52). Lismore parish is the only one in the diocese never at any time untied to any other parish. On the contrary two perpetual curacies, Cappoquin and Mocollop, were carved out of its extensive area, a sick call to parts of which 'might entail a thirty miles ride over unspeakable roads' (Power, *Waterford and Lismore*, p. 216).

3 Power, *Waterford and Lismore*, p. 49.

4 St. J.D. Seymour, *The diocese of Emly* (Dublin, 1913), p. 140.

5 Power, *Waterford and Lismore*, p. 52. In the diocese of Lismore rectories were impropriate only to dignitaries and prebendaries of the cathedral church and to laymen but in many Irish dioceses there were parishes and vicarages endowed in which the rectories were held also by clergymen who had no duties other than to receive the rectorial tithes.

6 A 'rectory entire' was a parish in which the rector was in holy orders and responsible for the cure of souls.

7 *Papers relating to the established church in Ireland*, p. 232, HC 1807, v; *3rd rep; 4th rep*, p. 737.

8 Clonegam, Donoughmore, Kiltegan, Irishlounaght, Monksland, Kilrush, Lisronagh, Mora, Outeragh, Mortlestown, Clonmel, Tullaghmelan (*4th rep*, pp 732–61).

9 Affane, Aglish, Ballymacart, Colligan, Dungarvan, Kilronan, Kinsalebeg, Lisgenan, Fews, Ringagoonagh, Rossmire, Stradbally, Clonea, Kilwatermoy, Kilcocken, Whitechurch and Lickoran (ibid.).

10 Tubrid, Ardmore, Derrygrath, Newcastle, Ballybacon, Kilmolash, Tullaghorton, Diser, Kilmolean, Kilgobinet, Kilrossanty, Modeligo, Siskinan, Clashmore and Kilbarrymeaden.

11 Quoted in Rennison, *Succession list*, p. 233.

12 *Papers relating to the established church in Ireland*, pp 222–33, HC 1807, v.

13 Register of the parish of Tullaghmelan among MSS in the possession of the rector of Clonmel. Yet Lewis, *Topographical dictionary* (1837), ii, p. 654 says it was 'erected about forty-six years since' while a triennial visitation book of 1844 quoted in Rennison, *Succession list*, p. 205 gives the date of its erection as 1813.

14 Rennison, *Succession list*, p. 195.

15 'That it may be learned how far the recommendations contained in the former report have been acted upon and proved effectual and particularly for securing to the people of Ireland the beneficial influence of the precept and example of an universally resident body of parochial clergy' (Address to the prince regent by the house of commons).

16 *Papers relating to the established church in Ireland*, pp 244–53, HC 1820, ix. Out of 45 benefices in the diocese of Ferns, only four were without churches (ibid.).

17 The vicar of Clashmore was stated to be 'not resident at present; but will reside when the new church shall be finished; he was lately collated to the prebend to make the living of sufficient value to reside on'. A grant had been obtained from the Ecclesiastical Commissioners in

1816 for building a new church at Killaloan but it was not completed until 1827 (Rennison, *Succession list*, p. 168). As suggested by Bishop Trench in 1807, Kinsalebeg and Lisgenan had been separated from Templemichael and Kilcocken (they were in any case, separated by the estuary of the river Blackwater). In 1746 Templemichael church had been in ruins while at Kinsalebeg there was 'a church built but going to decay'. In 1746 Templemichael church had been in ruins while at Kinsalebeg there was 'a church built but going to decay' (Smith, *County and city of Waterford*, p. 44). In 1819 the position was reversed; there was a church at Templemichael but 'no church yet' at Kinsalebeg. It was built in 1821 (*4th rep*, p. 747.).

18   *Papers relating to the established church in Ireland,* pp 246, 250, HC 1820, ix.

19   Ibid.

20   *4th rep*, pp 730–61.

21   Revd John Averill had in 1819 been holding the vicarage of Colligan and the prebend and vicarage of Clashmore together, as an inducement to him to take up residence at Clashmore where a new church was being built (*Papers relating to the established church in Ireland* p. 244 HC 1820 ix). But he died in 1820 and although the prebend and its vicarage continued to be held together, Colligan, then worth under £30 was nominally allowed to stand alone! From 1834 until its union with Whitechurch in 1841 it was held by the curate of Templemichael (Rennison, *Succession list*, p. 142). The Revd Daniel Sullivan in 1820 changed the place of his non-residence from Rathronan to Kilronan. He continued to live at Lismore where he was a vicar and preacher to the dean and chapter. After paying his curate at Rathronan £50, he himself only received £50 out of the living, but at Kilronan he had to pay a curate only £10 and thus himself received £175 a year (*Papers relating to the established church in Ireland*, p. 248, HC 1820, ix and *4th rep*, p, 744).

22   *Est. ch.*, pp 484–94.

23   It had a church population of 44 while Kilcash was left with only 10 (ibid.).

24   Ibid.

25   Under the Church Temporalities Act 3 & 4 Willian IV cap. 31.

26   Smith, *County and city of Waterford*, pp 43, 45, 46.

27   Ibid., pp 43, 44, 47. Throughout the 18th and 19th centuries Mothel was always above average – in 1746 it was worth £80 (p. 45).

28   Ibid., p. 47.

29   Rennison, *Succession list*, p. 56 and Smith, *County and city of Waterford*, p. 42.

30   Rennission, *Succession list*, p. 209 and Smith, *County and city of Waterford*, p. 47.

31   Rennison, *Succession list*, pp 130, 134.

32   *Paper relating to the established church in Ireland*, pp 222–33, HC 1807 V.

33   Mora, value about £150; Rossmire, value £140; Kilbarrymeaden, value £86; Colligan, not worth £30; Kilrossanty; Seskinan 'not being £100'; Rathronan, 'not worth £70'; Derrygrath 'not worth £160'.

34   *Papers relating to the established church in Ireland*, pp 244–53, HC 1820, ix.

35   Mora, Kilmolash, Kilbarrymeaden, Rossmine, Rathronan, Mortlestown, Newcstle (Co. Tipperary) and Derrygrath.

36   *4th rep*, pp 730–61.

37   The curate's stipend had of course to be taken out of the above incomes. 14 of the 41 benefices were under £150 a year but at the same period out of 10,480 benefices in England and Wales, 3528 were worth not more than £150 (Norman Sykes, *Church and state in England in the XVIIIth century* (Cambridge, 1934), p. 212) and unlike Ireland practically all these benefices would have had churches.

38   *Est. ch.*, pp 484–94.

39   *Est. ch.*, p. 721.

40   E.A. Stopford, *The income and requirements of the Irish church* (Dublin, 1853), p. 41.

41   A.T. Lee, *Facts respecting the present state of the church in Ireland* (3rd ed. London and Belfast, 1865), p. 10.

42   *4th rep*, p. 762.

43   *The census of Ireland for the year 1861,* part V. General rep., pp 232–7, 246–50 (3204–IV), HC 1863, lxi.

44   RCB, Rural deans' report, 1836. Yet this did not include 250 'dissenters' – probably Quakers in Clonmel.

45   *Est. ch.*, p. 32.

46 *Est. ch.*, Cloyne had 78 benefices and of these 13 had less than 20 members of the established church.
47 *Est. ch.*, p. 745.
48 Ibid., p. 96.
49 7 & 8 Geo. IV., cap. 43; 708.Vic., cap. 54; and 11 & 12 Vic., cap 41 formed the code regulating the union and division of parishes at the time of disestablishment. They had superseded the acts 14 & 15 Chas. II cap. 10 (Irish); 2 Geo. I cap. 14; and 10 Geo. I cap. 6.
50 Only nine benefices were in the bishop's gift, 13 were in the patronage of the duke of Devonshire; 11 in that of the crown; three in that of the marquess of Ormonde; two each in that of the marquess of Waterford and the vicar-choral; and one in that of trustees.

4. INCUMBENTS AND CURATES

1 In 1959 there were no titled clergymen in Ireland but 12 peers, five baronets and one peer's son were members of the general synod (*Irish church directory*). Lord John George Beresford was made deacon in 1795 and ordained priest in 1797. He received both orders in Dublin from his relative Archbishop Beresford of Tuam. He never seems to have served a curacy and in 1799 he was presented by the crown to the rectory of Clonegam – the family seat, Curraghmore was in the parish – and was also given the deanery of Clogher. During his two years as an incumbent in Lismore diocese, most of the parochial duties were done by another clergyman but Lord John George did manage to officiate at three baptisms in August 1799 and at a burial in March 1801 (Register of the parish of Clonegam 1741–1827). The living of Clonegam yielded £748 gross in 1831, *4th rep*, p. 734.
2 'The incumbents were simply country gentlemen of moderate or humble fortune', J.T. Ball, *The reformed church of Ireland* (London Dublin, 1886), p. 180. In 1835 five of the incumbents were justices of the peace but this was a smaller proportion than in most of the Irish dioceses (*A return of all the clergymen in the commission of the peace in Ireland*, p. 3 (102), HC 1835, xliv, 95).
3 *4th rep*, p. 386.

4 RCB, Rural dean's report, 1836.
5 RCB, Rural dean's report, 1836; *4th rep*, p. 763.
6 J.B. Leslie, *Ossory clergy and parishes* (Enniskillen 1933), p. 108.
7 Rennison, *Succession list*, p. 120.
8 Only six benefices had better income – Clonegam, Inishlounaght, Kilsheelan, Mothel, Clonmel, Stradbally, *4th rep*, pp 730–60.
9 RCB, Rural dean's report, 1836. Ballybacon vicarage whose tithe composition was £180 possessed no church and contained only one member of the established church, *4th rep*, p. 758 and RCB, Rural dean's report, 1836.
10 *Est. ch.*, p. 494.
11 TCD, MS 948, 18 May 1811. At the same period the annual income of the Roman Catholic priest of Stradbally was about £125 out of which he had to give his curate board and lodging and a yearly salary of £10 (Power, *Waterford and Lismore*, p. 384).
12 Sir John Power, 1st baronet of Tullamaine, Co. Tipperary, created 15 July 1836; married Harriett 3rd daughter of Gervais Parker Bushe of Kilfane MP (by Mary, sister of the Rt. Hon. Henry Grattan MP) (Burke, *Peerage, baronetage and knightage* (London, 1959), sub 'Power of Kilfane.'
13 F. Ochille, *A hand-book to the 'Holy Citie of Ardmore' county of Waterford* (Youghal 1853) p. 37. For a time he may also have had a home in England for in a chancery petition of 1850, Shaw v. the vicars-choral among MSS in the possession of the dean of Lismore, his address is given as 'Freshford near Bath'.
14 *2nd rep*, p. 230; *4th rep*, p. 744
15 Burke, *Peerage*.
16 His eldest son 'of Barrettstown and Clonmoyle, Co. Waterford' was a deputy lieutenant, high sheriff and justice of the peace and married the co-heiress of Gervaise Bushe D.L. of Glencairn Abbey, Lismore. A daughter married Henry Villiers-Stuart of Dromana, MP (Burke, *Peerage*). Next to the Beresfords, the Villiers-Stuarts were the foremost family of the county.
17 His third son, the Revd George Beresford Power was curate and then rector of Kilfane, Co. Kilkenny (the family seat) 1879–1931 (Leslie, *Ossory clergy and parishes*, pp 292–3).
18 Madden, *Memoir*, p. 251.

19 Burke, *Landed gentry of Ireland* (London, 1899), p. 199.

20 Dorothea Herbert, *Retrospections, 1770–1789* (London 1929), p. 4.

21 Ibid., p. 5.

22 Ibid., p. 20.

23 'His Lordship was nearly related to my Mother' (ibid., p. 9).

24 Although the archbishop was not himself resident in his diocese 'the clergy trembled at his Nod and few of them escaped a severe stricture at his Visitations' (ibid., p. 40).

25 Ibid., p. 30.

26 Ibid., p. 171.

27 Herbert, *Retrospections*, pp 338, 335, 364, 369. 377.

28 Ibid., p. 406.

29 Rennison, *Succession List*, pp 146, 64. Yet the *Irish Ecclesiastical Gazette* says he died in 1871 at the age of 96.

30 Leslie, *Ossory clergy and parishes*, p. 217. The net income of the benefice about 1831 was £587 (*3rd rep*).

31 St. J.D. Seymour, *The succession of parochial clergy in the united diocese of Cashel and Emly* (Dublin 1908), p. 33.

32 *2nd rep*, p. 262. *4th rep*, p.682.

33 Rennison, *Succession list*, pp 146, 190. Newtownlennan was held with Clonegam 1754–1867 although they were about five miles apart. In 1836 it had no Protestant parishioners (RCB, Rural dean's report, 1832) and yielded an income of £441 about 1831, *4th rep*, p. 734.

34 His father had been MP for Old Leighlin and his brother was created a baron in 1797 and Viscount Monck with the significant date 5 January 1801. His first cousin Elizabeth Monck was wife of the first marquess of Waterford (obit 1800) (Burke, *peerage, baronetage and Knightage* sub Monck). Although the King was patron of the living it is unlikely that the wishes of the Beresford family would be disregarded in the choice of their parish clergyman.

35 Register of the parish of Clonegam.

36 *4th rep*, p. 734. He lived at Coolfin just outside the boundary of Clonegam parish. After the death of G.S. Monck it was purchased as the glebe-house. In 1891 Coolfin townland was transferred from Kilmeaden parish to Clonegam (Rennison, *Succession list*, p. 195).

37 The vicarage of Ardbraccan worth £890 net about 1831, *3rd rep*, p. 152.

38 *Papers relating to the established church in Ireland*, pp 223–33, HC 1807, v.

39 Ibid.

40 Ibid.

41 Ibid.

42 *Papers relating to the established church in Ireland*, pp 244–53, HC 1820, ix.

43 *4th rep*, pp 732–61

44 *Return showing the number of parishes with their several incomes in the dioceses of Cashel, Emly, Waterford and Lismore* (156), 1864, xliv, 57–61; *Return showing the number of livings in each diocese and the value of each living*, pp 59–61 (267), HC 1864, xliv, 727–9.

45 *Return showing the number of livings in each diocese and the value of each living*,.

46 He was the third son of the 1st baron Ponsonby and grandson John Ponsonby speaker of the Irish house of commons. He was ordained deacon and priest in 1795; was prebendary of Tipper in St Patrick's Dublin 1795–1801; vicar of Kill and Lyons 1801–7; precentor of St Patrick's 1806–18; rector of Cleenish, diocese of Clogher 1810–13; rector of Carnew, diocese of Ferns 1813–21; dean of St Patrick's 1818; vicar of Coolock, diocese of Dublin 1821–8. He was presented to Tallow by his relative the duke of Devonshire, E. Maturin, *Brief memoirs of all the bishops of Derry* (Londonderry, 1867), p. 68. In 1806 he was 'generally resident on his other benefice in the diocese of Kildare' and in 1819 was returned as resident at St Patrick's deanery.

47 J.B. Leslie, *Derry clergy and parishes* (Enniskillen, 1937), p. 21, 'A man of talent, handsome, of courtly manners but lazy in business. He had but one vice, a passion for gambling, and notwithstanding his deanery and afterwards his bishopric, worth then £14,000 a year, he was always needy and dunned by creditors', Sir John Ponsonby, *The Ponsonby family* (London, 1929), p. 93.

48 *Papers relating to the established church in Ireland*, p. 228, HC 1807, v.

49 J.B. Leslie, *Armagh clergy and parishes* (Dundalk, 1911), p. 355. He was son of Revd Hugh Stewart, prebendary of Armagh cathedral and brother of Sir

Hugh Stewart, bart. of Athenry (Cotton, *Fasti* v, p. 205)

50 *Papers relating to the established church in Ireland*, p. 246, HC 1820, ix.

51 £681 net from Mothel, (*4th rep*, p. 748) and £1,318 net from Loughgilly (*3rd rep*, p. 74).

52 Leslie, *Armagh clergy and parishes*, p. 355.

53 *4th rep*, p. 746.

54 RCB, Rural deans' report, 1836

55 *Papers relating to the established church in Ireland*, p. 250, HC 1820, ix and *4th rep*, p. 731.

56 Cotton, *Fasti*, i, p. 176.

57 £426 as precentor of St Carthagh's (*2nd rep*, p. 198), £289 as incumbent of Ardfinnan union (*4th rep*, p. 730). £316 as rector of Kilmacow (*4th rep*, p. 548).

58 *Papers relating to the established church in Ireland*, p. 248, HC 1820, ix and *4th rep*., p. 746.

59 RCB, Rural dean's report, 1836.

60 *Papers relating to the established church in Ireland*, p. 143, HC 1820, ix.

61 *3rd rep*, p. 588; *4th rep*., p. 746.

62 Ibid.

63 *Papers relating to the established church in Ireland*, pp 159, 246, HC 1820, ix. The vicar of Dungarvan was paid £3 for the occasional duties. In 1836 there were only twelve church people (RCB, Rural dean's report, 1836).

64 *Returns relative to the clergy of Ireland*, p. 57 (246), HC 1824, xxi.

65 This is well illustrated in a statement of the registrar of the diocese in 1863: 'N.B. – Not one parish in the diocese, with a church in which there is not a clergyman resident in the glebe-house, if there be one or in the most convenient place in adjoining parish, and doing the duty of the parish', *Return showing the number of parishes with their several incomes in the dioceses of Cashel, Emly, Waterford and Lismore*, p. 3 (156), 1864, xliv, 69.

66 *Papers relating to the established church in Ireland*, pp 226, 330, HC 1807, v. Yet in 1811 one of these Dr Devereux of Stradbally was said to require a curate only because he was frequently obliged to leave his benefice, which had only nine Protestant families (TCD, MS 948).

67 *Papers relating to the established church in Ireland*, pp 222–33, HC 1807, v.

68 James Woodforde, *Diary of a country parson*, ed. John Beresford (London 1931), v, 386.

69 *Papers relating to the established church in Ireland*, pp 226–8 HC 1807, v.

70 *An account of the salaries and emoluments of curates in Ireland*, p. 18 (721), HC 1833, xxvii, 436.

71 In England in 1835 the average curate's stipend was £81 (Sykes, *Church and state in England*, p. 209). The pay of labourers was seven pence a day *circa* 1826 (Le Fanu, *Seventy years of Irish life*, p. 99).

72 Ibid.

73 Ibid. and Rennison, *Succession list*, pp 61, 152.

74 Rennison, *Succession list*, p. 143. Thomas Hudson resident curate of Templemichael at £75 was also non-resident vicar of Colligan (no church) at £43 a year.

75 *Est. ch.*, pp 484–94

76 The average curate's stipend for the whole country was £75, E.A. Stopford, *The income and requirements of the Irish church* (Dublin 1853), p. 41. Dr Johnson agreed with Boswell in 1777 that £100 was desirable for a curate but held that it was unattainable because of the poverty of benefices (Sykes, *Church and state in England*, p. 226).

77 Henry Newland, *An apology for the established church in Ireland* (Dublin 1829), p. 169.

78 Ibid., p. 215.

5. CHURCH BUILDINGS

1 They were the parish churches of Affane, Ardinnan, Ardmore, Cahir, Carrick, Clonegam, Clonmel, Disert, Dungarvan, Kinsalebeg, Mothel, Rathronan, Shanrahan, Tallow, Tubrid, and Whitechurch; Smith *County and city of Waterford*, pp 42–7.

2 William P. Burke, *History of Clonmel* (Waterford, 1907), p. 264.

3 Lewis, *Topographical dictionary*, i, p. 369.

4 Burke, *History of Clonmel*, p. 264.

5 Its dimensions were *Length*: nave 96 feet, choir 50 feet, north aisle 103 feet (5 bays). There were 4 bays on the south the fifth being occupied by the tower. *Width*: nave 23 feet, aisles 9 feet each, piers 2 feet 9 inches (ibid.).

6 Ibid., p. 270. The church had been re-pewed *c.*1796. (RCB, Triennial Visitation book 1796, copy by W.H. Rennison).

7 Burke, *History of Clonmel*, p. 271; Clonmel parish, 'Account of adjourned

meeting of parishioners 28 December 1855' in Vestry book 1808–60 among MSS in the possession of the rector of Clonmel.

8   Villages are not a natural phenomenon in Ireland. Any beautiful villages which we possess are usually the creation of the landlord e.g. Adare, Co. Limerick. In any case, Irish churches are placed on monastic sites associated with their patron not to serve centres of population that may have moved. This is especially so of the cathedral: Achonry is in the middle of a field without a dwelling in sight.

9   Of the 16 parish churches in 1746, only one survived the 19th century in anything like its original form.

10   Emily, countess of Kildare went to Maynooth church one Saturday morning in 1759 and noted 'the man told me I could not go to my own seat which was not ready for that no *quality* was ever expected at Church of a week day'. She also went on the following day, Brian Fitzgerald: *Emily, duchess of Leinster 1731–1814* (London and New York 1949), p. 67. Her attendance on a week day may have been unusual but now it would be unheard of even if there was a service to attend.

11   1741–1827, among MSS with the rector of Clonegam.

12   Ann, wife of James Power, third earl of Tyrone gave a chalice to Mothel church in 1697 and a paten in 1712–13 and a flagon to Carrrick church in 1715 (R. Wyse Jackson, 'Old church plate of Lismore diocese', *Journal of the Royal Society of Antiquaries of Ireland*, 85 (1955), pp 51–61. Thus it would appear that the Powers of Curraghmore worshipped either at Mothel distant about three miles or at Carrick about six miles away or at both. The third earl's only child Lady Catharine married in 1717 Sir Marcus Beresford, the builder of Clonegam who was created Viscount Tyrone in 1720 and earl in 1746.

13   Wyse Jackson, 'Old church plate'.

14   A list of Returns made by the clergy of the number of Protestants and papists quoted in Rennison, *Succession list*, p. 233.

15   *4th rep*, p. 353.

16   RCB, Visitation of 1836, Rural deans' report, 1836.

17   Rennison, *Succession list*, p. 189. A Memorial to the lord lieutenant and privy council to secure the necessary Act of parliament was signed by the rector and 19 Protestant parishioners including the marquess of Waterford who was one of the churchwardens (Vestry book, 17 Feb. 1851).

18   Deed of Endowment 1852 among MSS of the dean of Lismore.

19   Lewis, *Topographical dictionary*, ii, p. 673.

20   Rennison, *Succession list*, p. 221.

21   *3rd rep*, p. 18.

22   In Lismore diocese in 1836 there were 20 benefices with less than 50 Protestant parishioners (RCB, Rural deans' report, 1836); in 1861 there were 20 with less than 40, *Est. ch.*, p. 889.

23   Clonegam and Villierstown are special cases. See *supra*.

24   Power, *Waterford and Lismore*, p. 73.

25   'Vestry book for the parish of Ardmore and Ballymacart 1827' amongst MSS of the vicar of Dungarvan.

26   Power, *Waterford and Lismore*, p. 77; Smith, *County and city of Waterford*, p. 71.

27   Vestry book

28   Ibid.

29   Rennison, *Succession list*, p. 123.

30   TCD, MS 948.

31   Rennison, *Succession list*, p. 135.

32   Lewis, *Topographical dictionary*, i, p. 239.

33   The church of 1820 does not appear to have been regularly used after the union of the parish with Cappoquin in 1871 (Rennison, *Succession list*.) although it was not demolished until 1949 (*Year-book of the united dioceses of Cashel and Emly, Waterford and Lismore, 1950* (privately published, 1950).

34   TCD, MS 948. In 1796 the church was 'newly ceiled' (RCB, Triennial Visitation book, copy by W.H. Rennison). He seems however to have undergone a rapid change of mind for an Order of the Privy Council for changing the site of the parish church (pursuant to 21 George I 'An Act for the real union and division of parishes') mentions as a pre-requisite, that the bishop has given his consent (Order given at Dublin 15 October 1812 among MSS of the vicar of Cahir).

35   *4th rep*, p. 353.

36   Rennison, *Succession list* p. 129; RCB, Copy by W.H. Rennison of act of consecration.

37 Lewis, *Topographical dictionary*.
38 Information from the agent of the Cahir estates; RCB, Visitation, Rural deans' report, 1836.
39 J.D. Forbes, *Victorian architect, the life and work of William Tinsley* (Bloomington 1953), p. 19.
40 Kilrossanty (consecrated 1808) has a shallow apse. Ardmore (consecrated 1841) has transepts but they are so small as to be almost non-functional. Killaloan (consecrated 1827) had a chancel added early in the 20th century.
41 By 3 and 4 William IV, cap. 37.
42 Parish of Clonmel, vestry book, pp 217, 226; *Est. ch.*, pp 871–80.
43 Clonmel vestry book 14 February 1856.
44 *Annual report of the. ecclesiastical. commissioners of Ireland for year ending 1 August 1847*, p. 3 (10), HC 1847–8, xxix, 209.
45 Forbes, *Victorian architect*, pp 21, 35. The parish appears never before, even in the pre-reformation period to have had a church (Power, *Waterford and Lismore* p. 234).
46 Information from a descendant of George Wilson; *Year-book of the dioceses of Cashel and Emly, Waterford and Lismore, 1945*, (Privately published, 1945).
47 'They the churchwardens shall provide ... at the common charge of the parish two books of Common-Prayer; one for the minister and the other for the Clerk ... and likewise the Bible of the last Translation ... also a fit seat for the minister to read Service and a comely and decent pulpit ... a font of stone set in the antient usual place ... together with a fair Table ... and a cup of Silver ... Which Table shall stand covered in Time of Divine Service with a Carpet of Silk or other decent stuff ... and with a fair Linen Cloth at the Time of the Ministration, as becometh that Table' (canon xciv).
48 Carrick, Dungarvan, Lismore, Tallow, and Templemichael, Jackson, 'Old church plate').
49 Ardfinnan, Ardmore, Disert, Clonegam, Lismore, Rathronan, Shanrahan, Villierstown (chapel) and Whitechurch (ibid.). In addition the chalice and paten of Mothel, recently sold, although both were the gift of Anne, countess of Tyrone, dated respectively from 1697 and

1712–13. Affane has an odd chalice of 1719 and Cahir an odd paten of 1731 (ibid., pp 51 and 54). Yet in 1790 it was noted that both chalice and paten in Cahir were of block tin (RCB, Triennial Visitation book, copy by W.H. Rennison). Three of the 18th-century sets were the gift of Bishop Thomas Milles (1780–40) 'a High Church Tory' (Jackson, 'Old church plate'), which may explain why the inscriptions on his gifts were in Latin. The chalice that he gave to Ardfinnan was a re-modelling of older silver *addition quatror argenti anciis*.
50 RCB, Triennial visitation books
51 Ibid., 1790. In this year Cahir had only four pews, by 1796 it had three more.
52 Ibid., 1796. Mothel was also in very bad repair 'no windows but the East and in that fourteen panes broken.'
53 Ibid. Yet at this period the nearby church of Carrick was in very good order.
54 Ardfinnan, 'the Eastern window very bad, it is not likely to stand the winter'. Ardmore; Cahir 'roof leaks in many places'; Clonmel; Mothel 'Architect says roof must be stripped and re-slated and Shanrahan'. (RCB, Rural dean's report, 1836)
55 Tullaghmelan, Cappoquin, Tallow, Ardmore, Cahir, Ardfinnan, and Derrygrath (ibid.). This refers only to the books required on altar and reading desk.
56 Whitechurch, Ardmore, Clonmel, Cahir, and Derrygrath (ibid.). Of course this refers to the surplice that the parish was bound to provide. The incumbent probably would have his own, in addition.
57 Ibid.
58 'Vestry book of the Parish of Abbey 1804–72'. Among MSS with the rector of Clonmel.
59 RCB, Triennial visitation book; Parish of Clashmore, vestry book 1820–70, among MSS with the vicar of Dungarvan., Parish of Ardmore, vestry book, 1829; Parish of Clonmel, vestry book, 19 April 1824.
60 RCB, Rural dean's report, 1836. The cloth in question cannot have been 'the fair linen cloth' since 'the linen' was in good order. At Derryrath 'the covers of the communion table, pulpit and reading desk' were described as 'in a bad state' (ibid.).

61 RCB, Rennison, 'History of the united diocese 1746–1872'. For a discussion of the advantages and disadvantages of square pews see Addleshaw and Etchells, *The architectural setting of Anglican worship*, pp 86–98.

62 Parish of Clonmel, vestry book.

63 Parish of Carrick, vestry book 1813–1916, among MSS formerly with the vicar of Killaloan; Parish of Clonmel, vestry book; parish of Dungarvan, vestry book, among MSS with the vicar.

64 Parish of Clonmel, vestry book, 28 Dec. 1855, 25 Apr. 1836.

65 In 1855 Clonmel church had accommodation for 230 in galleries, 520 on the ground floor and 200 in back and front aisles and on forms in the gallery passages. The plan submitted by Welland provided for 707 sittings (21 inches each) or 774 (18 inches each) without the use of side galleries; with short side galleries 767 or 844 respectively could be accommodated (ibid.).

66 Ibid., 28 December 1855.

67 Vestry book.

68 Ibid.

69 RCB, Rennison, 'History of the united diocese, 1746–1872'; *Est. ch.*, p. 882; Parish of Ardmore, vestry book.

70 48 George III, cap. 65.

71 8 George I, cap. 11, 12 and 12 George III, cap. 16, 43; George III, cap. 158, and 47 George III, cap. 23.

72 3 and 4 William IV. cap. 37.

73 At Cahir, Disert and Tubrid. (RCB, Return of Simon Preston, deputy registrar of Waterford and Lismore, 20 January 1768, copy by W.H. Rennison) yet the date of the erection of Cahir glebe-house is given as 1816 in *4th rep*, p. 353. It seems unlikely that the existence of a former house would pass unnoticed.

74 Ardfinnan built in 1819 at a cost of £1477; Ardmore, date and cost unknown (not given in RCB, Return of Simon Preston, (1768) but Smith, *County and city of Waterford*, p. 43, records a house there); Cahir in 1816 at £1385; Carrick in 1816 at £618; Clashmore in 1826 at £831; Clonmel in 1806 at £1143; Disert in 1782 at £369; Kilrossanty in 1807 at £382; Kilrush (at Lismore) in 1795 at £554; Mothel in 1818 at £1303; Outeragh in 1825 at £659; Tubrid in 1793 at £625; Tullaghmelan in 1818 at £1014 (*4th rep*, pp 730–61) Lewis, *Topographical dictionary* gives slightly different figures.

75 By the addition of houses at Inishlounaght, Mocollop, Monksland, Rossmire, Shanrahan and Stradbally. Tallow is doubtful, *Est. ch*, pp 485–95.